Acclaim for *God's Healing Mercy*

God's Healing Mercy is a must-read for anyone who wants to encounter the living, joyful, and healing face of the Father of Mercy. By focusing on Divine Mercy in Scripture as well as the lives of the saints, you'll come to a deeper understanding of God's love for you and the healing His mercy is ready to provide."

—Dr. Scott Hahn
Author and Scripture Scholar

God's Healing Mercy is a gem, steeped in Sacred Scripture and Holy Tradition. Kathleen Beckman has provided us with the consolation of the Truth, who is Jesus. Mercy Incarnate beckons us through the pages of this book to return to Him and to not be afraid to say "yes" to His offer of merciful and superabundant healing of our minds and hearts, our bodies and souls. Read this book and be restored and strengthened in your faith, hope and charity.

—Most Reverend David Kagan
Bishop of Bismarck Diocese, North Dakota

God's Healing Mercy is a praiseworthy work. Kathleen Beckman has done a superb job of illustrating the deep mercy of God while assisting and even challenging the reader to engage in personal reflection at the end of each chapter. In addition to being edified by the several "profiles in mercy" contained in the book, the user should experience a profound sense of hope and a deeper understanding of the healing power of Divine Mercy.

—Monsignor Stephen Doktorczyk
Official at the Holy See, Vatican City State

An inspired work on the triumph of God's healing mercy! As illustrated in this book, authentic mercy, when encountered through humility, sets us free from the bondage of our own sin and in turn allows us to

D0595686

set others free through our own expression of God's love and forgiveness. The scriptural exercises in Beckman's book lead you to a healing encounter with the Father of Mercy. Mercy is illumined by two realities; the first is that we are sinners in need of forgiveness, and the second is that God is always merciful when we recognize our failings, our needs, and turn to Him for His healing touch.

—**Daniel Burke**
Executive Director, *National Catholic Register*, A Service of EWTN

A wonderful book that is rich in insight and inspiration! Written in time for the Jubilee Year of Mercy, *God's Healing Mercy* will have perennial value. In a world that misunderstands mercy—thinking it means condoning harm or killing those who suffer or not having to do anything because God always forgives—Kathleen Beckman offers practical advice from her own experience and numerous sources that show us how to find healing and peace through the practice of mercy. The stories about mercy in action and "God's Letter to You" from the writings of St. Faustina, St. Pio, and others are especially helpful.

—**Father James Kubicki, S.J.**
Best-selling author, National Director of the Apostleship of Prayer

A remarkable book! Pope Francis has invited the world into a deep encounter with the wounds of Christ, where our own wounds will be healed. What does this look like? How is this done? *God's Healing Mercy* is a practical guide to giving ourselves over to Divine Mercy, which makes all the difference here and for eternity. I will be giving this book to many people.

—**Kathryn Jean Lopez**
National Review Online

Kathleen Beckman's use of the image of "rays of mercy" flooding so many situations of human need, coupled with powerful words from saints and recent popes, provides a profound resource for all those desiring to receive the merciful love of God in a deeper way. Prayerfully reading *God's Healing Mercy* will transform many hearts and lives.

—**Rev. Richard J. Gabuzda**
Executive Director, The Institute for Priestly Formation

God's Healing Mercy is an invitation to a healing encounter with the mercy of the Father. Beckman writes with compassion, imparting wisdom gained from her personal experiences, which will open doors for you to look at your life from the Lord's merciful heart. This book will help you to be liberated from those things that hold you back from receiving God's merciful love.

—**Rev. John Rozembajgier**
Vice-Rector of the College of Liberal Arts,
Pontifical College Josephinum

God's Healing Mercy is a timely work that testifies to the healing power of divine mercy. Through the use of Sacred Scripture and the lives of the saints, Beckman reiterates that the Father's mercy is a way of life and healing medicine. Readers are led on a path to deeper understanding of the transformative gift of divine mercy.

—**Bryan Thatcher M.D.**
Founder Eucharistic Apostles of Divine Mercy

.

God's Healing Mercy

Also by Kathleen Beckman
from Sophia Institute Press:

Praying for Priests:
A Mission for the New Evangelization

KATHLEEN BECKMAN, L.H.S.

GOD'S HEALING
MERCY

Finding Your Path to
Forgiveness, Peace, and Joy

SOPHIA INSTITUTE PRESS
Manchester, New Hampshire

The Scripture citations used in this work are from the *Second Catholic Edition of the Revised Standard Version of the Bible* (RSV), copyright © 1965, 1966, and 2006 by the Division of Christian Education of the National Council of the Churches of Christ in the United States of America. Used by permission. All rights reserved.

Excerpts from the *Catechism of the Catholic Church*, Second Edition, for use in the United States of America, copyright © 1994 and 1997, United States Catholic Conference—Libreria Editrice Vaticana. Used by permission. All rights reserved.

Imprimatur: ✠ Most Reverend Kevin W. Vann, J.C.D., D.D.
Bishop of Orange, September 23, 2015

Sophia Institute Press
Box 5284, Manchester, NH 03108
1-800-888-9344

www.SophiaInstitute.com

Sophia Institute Press® is a registered trademark of Sophia Institute.

Library of Congress Cataloging-in-Publication Data

Beckman, Kathleen.
    God's healing mercy : finding your path to forgiveness, peace, and joy / Kathleen Beckman, L.H.S.
        pages cm
    Includes bibliographical references.
    ISBN 978-1-62282-315-4 (pbk. : alk. paper) 1. God (Christianity)—Mercy. 2. Catholic Church—Doctrines. 3. Mercy—Biblical teaching. 4. Mercy. 5. Forgiveness—Religious aspects—Christianity. 6. Forgiveness of sin. 7. Spiritual life—Catholic Church. 8. Christian saints. I. Title.
    BT153.M4B43 2015
    231'.6—dc23

                                                                                    2015032508

First printing

To Fr. Raymond Skonezny, S.T.L., S.S.L.,
my spiritual father and teacher of twenty-five years

To Ella Simone Beckman, our first grandchild,
whom we entrust to God's mercy

*Do we believe that Jesus can heal us
and bring us back from the dead?*

—Pope Francis

Contents

Foreword

There are many inspiring accounts of events involving St. John Vianney, the patron saint of priests. As pastor (curé) of the parish in Ars, France, besides teaching, preaching, and caring for the poor, he would be in the confessional for eleven to sixteen hours per day. One day a woman made her way to the parish. Seeing lines of people waiting to go to confession, she asked one of them the estimated wait time. "About three days" was the reply. The woman could not wait, so she made her way into the church and up to the Communion rail, where she got down on her knees and began to pray. The saintly pastor finished the confession he was hearing and excused himself to the next penitent. He walked over to the woman and said, "He will be saved."

The woman did not believe him. It turns out that the distressed woman's husband had been an official in the French Revolution. He arrived at the point of despair, made his way to a bridge, jumped off, and died shortly after hitting the water below. So she was rightly concerned about his eternal salvation. St. John Vianney explained that between the bridge and the water, the man had made an Act of Contrition. The widow was understandably baffled, as her husband had not lived a Catholic life on earth.

The curé asked her, "Do you remember when you put up the shrine to our blessed Mother in your home?"

"Yes," she replied.

"Did he stand in the way?"

"No," she responded.

"Well, it was through that act of openness that the Lord worked and prompted him just before his death to make that Act of Contrition."

Not only should this story give us hope; it also should serve as a powerful example of the Lord's boundless mercy, which He offered from the beginning of His public ministry. He invites us to respond to it. It seems He also gives us reminders along the way. A more recent example comes in the form of Jesus appearing to a Polish nun, Faustina Kowalska, beginning not long before the commencement of World War II. In this series of apparitions, Jesus told Sr. Faustina that He desired to inaugurate a great time of Divine Mercy — to pour out his merciful love on the world in an unprecedented way. Jesus told Sr. Faustina:

> In the Old Covenant, I sent prophets wielding thunderbolts to My people. Today I am sending you with My mercy to the people of the whole world. I do not wish to punish aching mankind, but I desire to heal it, pressing it to My Merciful Heart.

Jesus even asked Faustina to have the image of His Divine Mercy painted for the entire world to see — Jesus clothed in white with rays of red and white shining forth from His merciful heart, symbolizing the blood and water that flowed from the Savior's side. It is this Divine Mercy, flowing from the heart burning with love for all humanity, that Jesus desires to pour out upon the world in this great time of Divine Mercy.

This time of Divine Mercy intensified when, from the same country of Poland, still struggling under the rule of atheistic communism, God raised up St. John Paul II, a pope of mercy. As Archbishop of Kraków, Karol Wojtyła was fully aware of the Divine Mercy messages Sr. Faustina had received from Jesus, and mercy was an important theme of his pontificate. In 1980, the Supreme Pontiff wrote his encyclical on Divine Mercy, *Dives in Misericordia*, or "Rich in Mercy." In this encyclical, the pope insisted that Divine Mercy is not only the answer to the many ills of humanity today but the very mission of the Church, and each of her members is to be an instrument of Divine Mercy to all we encounter. He stated:

> Modern man often anxiously wonders about the solution to the terrible tensions which have built up in the world and which entangle humanity.... In the name of Jesus Christ crucified and risen, in the spirit of His messianic mission, enduring in the history of humanity, we raise our voices and pray that the Love which is in the Father may once again be revealed at this stage of history, and that, through the work of the Son and Holy Spirit, it may be shown to be present in our modern world and to be more powerful than evil: more powerful than sin and death. (no. 15)

In fact, the mission of Divine Mercy was so at the heart of St. John Paul II's papacy that in the year 2000 he canonized Sr. Faustina, proclaiming the Second Sunday of Easter as Divine Mercy Sunday, fulfilling a specific request that Jesus made to Sr. Faustina.

Pope Francis recently called for a Year of Mercy, writing:

> Mercy is the very foundation of the Church's life. All of her pastoral activity should be caught up in the tenderness

she makes present to believers; nothing in her preaching and in her witness to the world can be lacking in mercy. The Church's very credibility is seen in how she shows merciful and compassionate love.... The time has come for the Church to take up the joyful call to mercy once more. It is time to return to the basics and to bear the weaknesses and struggles of our brothers and sisters. Mercy is the force that reawakens us to new life and instills in us the courage to look to the future with hope. (*Misericordiae Vultus*, 10)

The Jubilee Year of Mercy calls each of us to open our hearts to accept and experience God's mercy, which heals and brings peace. In *God's Healing Mercy*, you will be led to an encounter with merciful love. Enter the pages of the book wherein you will find the example of many saints who, like St. John Vianney, discovered the path of Divine Mercy to be one of true joy, peace, and healing.

Those of us who are pastors or involved in pastoral ministry at any level have all had experiences of the necessity and gift of God's mercy in our lives and the lives of those whom we serve. This can certainly be my testimony of thirty-four years of being a Catholic priest (including ten as bishop) and why I am grateful for Kathleen's writings here. This is a very readable and understandable synthesis of the reality of the gift that is Divine Mercy, well articulated in the lives of the saints and our Holy Fathers Saint John Paul II and Francis.

—Most Rev. Kevin W. Vann, JCD, DD
Bishop of Orange

PREFACE

Merciful Providence

✠

A year ago the magnanimous team at Sophia Institute Press released my book *Praying for Priests: A Mission for the New Evangelization.* To accompany the book, and with support from the Holy See, a team of priests and lay leaders launched a new apostolate: Foundation of Prayer for Priests (www.foundationforpriests.org). Consequently a good amount of time has been spent traveling in response to the demand for conferences and retreats for laity and priests. I have lost count of the number of cities and countries that I visited because of the interest in priestly renewal, intercessory prayer, and spiritual motherhood and fatherhood. Over the past year I have met incredibly generous Catholics who love our priests and desire to embrace the important call to spiritual motherhood and fatherhood for clergy.

I had cleared my calendar for the month of June to attend an event in Rome, but the event was postponed. I joyfully thought Providence arranged to give me a vacation in June!

The second week of May 2015, I led a diocesan priest retreat in Montana and then flew to Ave Maria University to speak at the Marian Eucharistic Conference. I settled into the University condo near the beautiful Ave Maria Oratory to pray and prepare for my opening presentation.

Then an e-mail arrived from Charlie McKinney, president of Sophia Institute Press: "Would you be interested in working on a new book related to the Year of Mercy? We'd have to move quickly." It was May 15, 2015, with the Year of Mercy beginning on December 8, 2015, and Charlie needed time to produce the book. Could I write a book on God's mercy in about two months? Previous books took years to write. After prayer with my spiritual director, I accepted Sophia's invitation. It required me to research, pray, and write full time in June and July. What I thought was to be a vacation was to be spent absorbed in the work of God's mercy. Providence provides, but sacrifice is necessary too.

Divine Mercy Required the Sacrifice of a Priest

The Lord also required the sacrifice of a suffering priest for this book. At this writing, the priest, who generously served as my spiritual director from 1992 to 2008, hangs between life and death in the cardiac intensive care unit at Hoag Hospital in Newport Beach, California. He is my spiritual father, the priest who I believe helped save my marriage and family after two traumatic events that nearly tore us apart. This priest has been like the Divine Physician for my family. When I told Father about this book, he was overjoyed.

Together we led prayerful pilgrimages to Poland; twice we visited the shrine of Divine Mercy in Kraków. With Magnificat we organized annual diocesan Divine Mercy conferences drawing several thousand attendees. The last conference occurred on the weekend that Pope John Paul II died, the vigil of Divine Mercy

Sunday 2005. That evening I hosted dinner at my home for the renowned speakers who arrived for the conference. Together we shared in the unforgettable experience of the passing of the Divine Mercy Pope, John Paul II.

Father Raymond Skonezny, S.T.L., S.S.L., entered the hospital for open-heart surgery on June 10, 2015. Eight weeks later, he remains in intensive care due to complications. He has nearly died twice. I've spent these weeks writing, praying, and visiting Father in the hospital as often as possible. Writing this book has been an intense labor of love.

Once when I visited Father while he was on intravenous morphine, I wanted to see how lucid he was after surgery. I said, "Father, I'm on chapter ten of twelve of the mercy book." Immediately he replied, "Oh, yes—divine mercy! It is all about God's amazing mercy! Tell everyone! Mercy—we all need God's mercy. Mercy makes everything beautiful." His enthusiasm flowed from a mystical experience of Divine Mercy when he flat-lined and almost died. Father saw the red and white rays of Divine Mercy flowing from the heart of Jesus during the time that his heart stopped. Also, he experienced the truths we profess in the Creed. He was surprised when he awoke, still on earth (due to emergency medical care).

Recently when two Norbertine priests from St. Michael's Abbey celebrated the Holy Sacrifice of the Mass in Father's ICU room, he suddenly awoke from a three-day coma. At the precise time of the Consecration of the Eucharist, Father began praying the prayers of the Consecration that he has prayed daily for fifty years of priesthood. He never slipped into a coma again after that special Mass.

I have finished this task entrusted to me. Sometimes I wrote through tears of grief over the intense suffering of my spiritual father. Father Skonezny has offered up his physical agony for this work that you, dear reader, may receive God's healing mercy.

If that were not enough, there is another priest, Monsignor Stephen Doktorczyk, without whom this book would not have been completed on time. Working from his office in Rome, he has been an editor, theologian, and intercessor in the development of this book. Monsignor Doktorczyk was a seminarian in Rome at the time of the Pontificate of the Polish Pope and is his spiritual son. On pilgrimage to Poland in 2011, we prayed at the shrine of Divine Mercy in Kraków.

If that were not enough, another spiritual son of St. John Paul II, Father John Rozembajgier, offered several inspirations for this work. Father Rozembajgier placed the manuscript on altars at miraculous shrines including Ars, Chartres, Lourdes, Fátima, Lisieux, Ávila, and the Miraculous Medal during his group pilgrimage of healing in Europe—asking the Lord to let the rays of healing mercy bless the readers of this work.

With all that Christ required to produce this book, I'm confident that He has special grace in store for you. May these pages lead you to *encounter God's healing mercy*!

—Kathleen Beckman, L.H.S.
August 28, 2015
Memorial of St. Augustine

How to Use This Book

This work is designed to be a guide for personal reflection or a group retreat. It includes spiritual exercises for inner healing based on God's mercy in Sacred Scripture and in the lives of the saints.

Ten Rules of Life
for Merciful Discipleship

1. I will decide to believe and trust in God's mercy.

2. I will live the present moment in Christ's merciful love.

3. I will hold firmly to one secret of mercy: prayer.

4. I will see in the holy Eucharist my only power and source of mercy.

5. I will have the wisdom of mercy: the science of the cross.

6. I will be faithful to my mission in the Church as a witness to Divine Mercy.

7. I will seek the peace the world cannot give and rest in God's merciful love.

8. I will carry out a holy mission by renewal in the Spirit and works of mercy.

9. I will speak one language and wear one uniform: mercy.

10. I will have one unique love: Mary, Mother of Mercy.

Marian Prelude

Mary, Mother of Mercy, Prepares the Way for Healing
Without Mary's cooperation with grace, we would not have the Divine Mercy. Mary not only gives us Jesus, but she also helps us to listen with our hearts, hear His voice, and receive His grace. Mary helps us rediscover God's healing mercy. Sitting at the feet of Jesus the Teacher is foundational for a healing encounter.

+ Mary's faith helps to heal our unbelief.

+ Mary's humility helps to heal our pride.

+ Mary's receptivity helps to heal our resistance.

+ Mary's hope helps to heal our discouragement.

+ Mary's love helps to heal our brokenness.

+ Mary's mercy helps to heal our wounds.

+ Mary's courage helps us to slay our Goliaths (see 1 Sam. 17).

Contemplatives in Action: Listeners and Soldiers

Mary, Mother of Mercy, is the model *contemplative in action*. The Virgin Mary knows how to sit at the feet of the Master, how to attune her heart to the Father's divine will, and how to abide in her Spouse, the Holy Spirit. Listening to God is foundational to becoming a soldier for Christ. Discipleship is a battle; prayer is the glue of our spiritual armor. Who better than Mary can help us receive the fullness of the Divine Mercy?

Modern life is filled with distractions that wear us down. Mary helps us to become contemplatives in action: *listeners and soldiers for Christ*. Our Lady beckons us to retreat in prayer with her Son Jesus so He can bless, enlighten, heal, and strengthen us for the journey. Jesus invites us to receive His merciful love for *healing, holiness, and happiness*.

Whether you read this book for inspiration or use it as a guide for a personal or group retreat so that you might receive the abundant grace that God has for you, I now have the joy of introducing you to *your* unique retreat team.

Your Personal Retreat Team

+ The Eternal Father, who holds you in His almighty hand

+ Jesus, your Divine Physician, Healer, and Restorer

+ The Holy Spirit, your Divine Retreat Master, Sanctifier

+ Mary, your merciful Mother who *prepares, protects, partners, prays*

+ Saints in this book, your intercessory team

Grace to Ask For

+ To accept the healing mercy of the Father's blessing

+ To receive the healing rays of Jesus' merciful heart

+ To accept the Holy Spirit's gifts of mercy in order to be set free for more love

+ To become a new creation with a servant heart like the Virgin Mary

+ To become, like the saints, a vessel of divine mercy for others

Opening Prayers

The Memorare

Remember, O most gracious Virgin Mary, that never was it known that anyone who fled to thy protection, implored thy help, or sought thy intercession was left unaided. Inspired by this confidence, I fly unto thee, O Virgin of virgins, my mother; to thee do I come, before thee I stand, sinful and sorrowful. O Mother of the Word Incarnate, despise not my petitions, but in thy mercy hear and answer me. Amen.

Cardinal Mercier Prayer to the Holy Spirit

I am going to reveal to you the secret of sanctity and happiness. Every day for five minutes, control your imagination and close your eyes to all the noises of the world in order to enter into yourself. Then, in the sanctuary of your baptized soul (which is the temple of the Holy Spirit) speak to that Divine Spirit, saying to Him:

O Holy Spirit, Beloved of my soul, I adore You. Enlighten me, guide me, strengthen me, console me. Tell me what I should do; give me Your orders. I promise to submit myself to all that You desire of me and to accept all that You permit to happen to me. Let me only know Your will.

If you do this, your life will flow along happily, serenely, and full of consolation, even in the midst of trials. Grace will be proportioned to the trial, giving you the strength to carry it, and you will arrive at the Gate of Paradise, laden with merit. This submission to the Holy Spirit is the secret of sanctity.

Saint Faustina on the Fruits of Prayer
A soul should be faithful to prayer despite torments, dryness, and temptations; because oftentimes the realization of God's great plans depends mainly on such prayer. If we do not persevere in such prayer, we frustrate what the Lord wanted to do through us or within us. Let every soul remember these words: And being in anguish, He prayed longer (*Diary*, no. 872).

Photo credits

1

RAYS OF DIVINE MERCY ON YOU

Healing from Unforgiveness to Forgiveness

✠

*At times how hard it seems to forgive!
And yet, pardon is the instrument placed
into our fragile hands to attain serenity of heart.*

—Pope Francis, *Bull of Indiction of the
Extraordinary Jubilee Year of Mercy*, 9

The Lord has provided an ocean of mercy for you. Therefore, your every action should be born of merciful love because the Father has been merciful to you. The psalmist proclaims God's healing mercy: "He forgives all your iniquity, he heals all your diseases, he redeems your life from the pit, he crowns you with mercy and compassion" (cf. Ps. 103:3–4).

When you dream of being loved; it is Jesus whom you seek. He has loved you first. His merciful arms reach out to you. Echo the humble prayer of the publican, "God, be merciful to me a sinner" (Luke 18:13).

IN THIS CHAPTER

+ We will reflect on what is true mercy and true forgiveness.

+ We will consider how divine mercy manifests itself in the forgiveness of sins, the healing power of Confession.

+ We will learn that a merciful heart is free of the poison of unforgiveness.

The burden of the heart in need of healing is real and urgent. The eternal Father manifested the extravagance of merciful love by sending to earth *our Healer*, His Son Jesus. Divine mercy makes straight our crooked ways.

Growing populations of people have no awareness of the need for God's mercy. Too many are desensitized to sin, forgetful of the need for repentance and forgiveness.

St. John Paul II explains, "The present day mentality, more perhaps than that of people of the past, seems opposed to a God of mercy, and in fact tends to exclude from life and to remove from the human heart the very idea of mercy."[1] The rebellious world situation makes the plea for divine mercy urgent. The Church beckons us to cry out full throated to God to open the floodgates of mercy upon aching humanity. Our hope lies in divine mercy for healing global festering wounds. His mercy is intimately personal and universally transformative. When you enter into the ocean of

---

[1] Pope John Paul II, *Dives in Misericordia* (*Rich in Mercy*), November 30, 1980, no. 2.

divine mercy for healing, others will be inspired to do the same. Like Lazarus, Christ calls you forth to new life.

What Is True Mercy?

A quite comprehensive presentation on the meaning of Divine Mercy is found in Pope John Paul II's encyclical letter *Dives in Misericordia (Rich in Mercy)*. The Holy Father makes two highly significant statements about God's mercy. First, mercy is love's second name. Secondly, mercy is the greatest attribute of God. Divine mercy is the tender, magnanimous love that willingly takes on another's suffering and pain. Mercy reaches out in a way that does not humiliate but instead restores to value the human person. It is love that does not allow itself to be conquered by pain, suffering, or evil. Mercy overcomes evil with good. It is the love that is more powerful than sin and death. On the Cross, Christ's heart was moved to mercy for a guilty criminal. Dismas, the Good Thief, stole Paradise by *accepting* divine mercy. To accept God's mercy requires the humility of a child

Mary's Magnificat proclaims, "His mercy is on those who fear[2] him from generation unto generation" (Luke 1:50). This scripture contains a *promise* and a *condition* about divine mercy. Mercy always brings hope, but it is not a blanket of false acceptance that

---

[2] Fr. John Hardon defines *fear of the Lord* as an "infused gift of the Holy Spirit that confirms the virtue of hope and inspires a person with profound respect for the majesty of God. Its corresponding effects are protection from sin through dread of offending the Lord, and a strong confidence in the power of his help." John Hardon, S.J., *Modern Catholic Dictionary*, s.v. "gift of fear," CatholicCulture.org, accessed August 19, 2015, https://www.catholicculture.org/culture/library/dictionary/.

no longer challenges us to live virtuously. God's mercy cannot be presumed, nor does it mean the absence of accountability, justice, or correction, or that anything goes because all will be forgiven. Mercy enables us to acknowledge and confront our weaknesses. It beckons us to turn away from sin and go back to Jesus.

The human heart agonizes, twists, and turns as it encounters pain and suffering, sin, loss, and death along the path of life. In the wake of pain we search for a remedy. We learn that the remedy is not found in ourselves. What we long for, and are made for, is Jesus, the Merciful One.

What Is True Forgiveness?

By the shedding of His blood on Calvary, Jesus forever changed the "eye for an eye" worldview. Jesus Christ is not only the *discoverer of forgiveness* in human affairs, but also the essence of forgiveness. "Forgiveness is a willingness to abandon one's right to resentment, negative judgment, and indifferent behaviour toward one who unjustly injured us, while fostering the undeserved qualities of compassion, generosity, and even love toward him or her."[3] This definition by a health professional fits Christ's gospel of forgiveness. It reminds us of the lives of the saints who exemplified forgiveness, such as Maria Goretti, Rita, John Paul II, and others.

Forgiveness is an opportunity to rise to the level of merciful love in imitation of Jesus, who forgives us countless times. When we break through and forgive, we often experience healing, peace, and freedom. To admit our faults, seek God's forgiveness,

---

[3] Robert Enright and Joanna North, *Exploring Forgiveness* (Madison, WI: University of Wisconsin Press, 1998), 26.

ask forgiveness of someone, and forgive ourselves requires true humility and grace. Forgiveness does not demand that we endure abuse or violence. If you hurt, acknowledge the hurt; do not bury the emotions; seek help. Bring your situation to prayer, counsel, and Confession (the desire for revenge, for example). We need, and God desires for us, to acknowledge wrongdoing. Forgiveness is not lowering ourselves to the base level of retaliation. Forgiveness is:

+ not condoning
+ not excusing
+ not tolerating
+ not forgetting
+ not reconciliation
+ not letting the offender "off the hook"
+ not a legal pardon

There are stages of forgiveness:

+ denial
+ self-blame
+ victim stage
+ indignation stage
+ survivor stage
+ integration stage

For pastoral care, we distinguish between:

+ the broken heart that feels it cannot forgive
+ the hardened heart that is determined not to forgive
+ the broken heart that is in need of healing
+ the hardened heart that is in need of conversion

The Primacy of Forgiveness

Christ placed the primacy of forgiveness within the perfect prayer that He taught His apostles, the Our Father. This familiar Christian prayer rolls off our tongue readily. Do we realize what we are praying? In the Our Father, we stand before God as forgiven and forgiving people. Forgiveness is less about sin than it is about restoring our relationship with God and others: "as we forgive those who trespass against us" (Matt. 6:12).

> This "as" is not unique in Jesus' teaching: "You, therefore, must be perfect, *as* your heavenly Father is perfect"; "Be merciful, even *as* your Father is merciful"; "A new commandment I give to you, that you love one another, even *as* I have loved you, that you also love one another." It is impossible to keep the Lord's commandment by imitating the divine model from outside; there has to be a vital participation, coming from the depths of the heart, in the holiness and the mercy and the love of our God. Only the Spirit by whom we live can make "ours" the same mind that was in Christ Jesus. Then the unity of forgiveness becomes possible and we find ourselves "forgiving one another, as God in Christ forgave" us. (CCC 2842)

Every act of forgiveness is life giving and leads to the discovery of another ray of God's mercy. When we accept God's forgiveness, we magnify the healing mercy of God. A merciful heart reflects the beauty of God in the world.

Like the prodigal son, when we bring ourselves in humility and contrition before the Father of Mercy, we are met with open arms. God transforms our wounds into trophies of love. Forgiveness is one of the most glorious, unique truths of Catholicism.

A merciful heart can enjoy unencumbered intimacy with God and others.

Divine Mercy Manifests Itself in the Forgiveness of Sins

The Church teaches that sins forgiven in the sacrament of Confession are actually removed from the soul (cf. John 20) and not merely covered over by Christ's merits. The Precious Blood is a divine stain remover for the fabric of the sinner's soul! Scripture teaches that *"all* have sinned and fall short of the glory of God" (Rom. 3:23; emphasis added). And in Proverbs, "for a righteous man falls seven times, and rises again" (Prov. 24:16).

Some people have a personal awareness of being sinners, of the need to ask for God's forgiveness, and of the necessity of mercy for healing spiritual wounds. This awareness comes as a gift of the Holy Spirit, who convicts us of the truth. Our part is to repent, offer reparation, avoid the near occasion of sin, seek help for sin addictions such as pornography, aim for continuing conversion, live a virtuous life, and frequent the sacraments, especially Confession.

According to St. Thomas Aquinas, the deepest root of sin is inordinate self-love.[4] How does this relate to accepting God's forgiveness? If I refuse the gift of God's mercy, am I not placing

---

[4] St. Thomas Aquinas, *Summa Theologica* I-II, Q. 77, art. 4; Q. 84, art. 4; quoted in Msgr. Charles Pope, "What Is the Deepest Root of Sin? It's Not in Your Wallet, and It's Much Closer Than You Might Think," *Community in Mission*, May 20, 2015, accessed August 19, 2015, http://blog.adw.org/2015/05/what-is-the-deepest-root-of-sin-its-not-in-your-wallet-and-its-a-lot-closer-than-you-might-think/.

my will and sin above God's will and divine mercy? Christ's salvific mission is about the forgiveness of sin — Adam and Eve's, yours and mine. The misery of the prodigal children of God is no match for the infinite mercy of God. Surrender to divine mercy!

A Personal Act of Mercy: Forgiveness and Healing

Accepting God's forgiveness may be the most difficult of all. If we have absorbed the thinking of the world in terms of being successful, how can we accept that our failures can lead us straight into the heart of Jesus, who mercifully "works all things together for good" (cf. Rom. 8:28)?

Mercy becomes of greater importance when we personally have need of it. In the times when we cry out from the depths of our agony, when our heart is broken, and when we have no one to cling to, His mercy envelops us. Suddenly we can perceive a new dawn, a fresh perspective, renewed strength, and the truth that we are redeemed, saved, healed by God. This is the truth that sets us free. Only in Christ can we perceive that we are truly lovable.

Our true identity is discovered through the eyes of God's mercy, not in the opinions of others, worldly standards, or demonic falsehood. Divine mercy enables us to let go of the past (confessed sin, repented offenses, false perceptions, repeated lies and injuries). The ocean of mercy will absorb these so that we can move forward in praise of His mercy. Not a few people journey in life with the unnecessary weight of *forgiven sins* impeding their freedom to love. Jesus exhorts: "shake off the dust from your feet" (Matt. 10:14). Reflect: I've fallen, I've been forgiven, and I go forward, my trust in His mercy.

The Balm of Mercy for Our Wounds

God's provision for the suffering we cause one another is forgiveness: a graced decision of the will to accept God's mercy and give it to others. In this way, we become healed healers. Sometimes letting go of unforgiveness seems almost impossible. The negative memories, the wounds from decades ago can haunt us still. Introspection alone is not helpful for healing. We tend to review the injury repeatedly without any benefit. What is *always* helpful for healing the wounds of unforgiveness is to ask for the revelation of God's love for the person who hurt us so that we may see the person and the situation in a new light.

Spiritual wounds, like a low-grade fever, are invisible yet very real and painful, and they leave us in need of divine medicine. Where is this divine medicine found? The Precious Blood is our healing medicine. From Christ's heart wound gushed the fountain of mercy, forming seven streams of sacramental healing.[5]

The Church's Healing Acts of Mercy

Sacramental Confession is one of the most intimate healing encounters with Divine Mercy. Jesus spoke to St. Faustina: "When you approach the confessional, know this, I am only hidden by the priest, but I myself act in your soul."[6] Forgiveness of our sins costs Jesus everything. He gave His life so that we would be able

---

[5] The seven sacraments of the Catholic Church are Baptism, Confirmation, Eucharist, Holy Communion, Confession, Marriage, Anointing of the Sick, and Holy Orders.

[6] *Diary of St. Maria Faustina Kowalska: Divine Mercy in My Soul* (Stockbridge, MA: Marian Press, 2014), no. 1602.

to confess our sins and receive absolution. How is it that we are afraid to receive such loving mercy as often as possible?

Some of the deepest inner healing I've experienced began with the words, "Forgive me, Father, for I have sinned." With the words of absolution, the plentitude of mercy had set me free. Revival is found in the confessional.

> The Lord Jesus Christ, physician of our souls and bodies, who forgave the sins of the paralytic and restored him to bodily health, has willed that his Church continue, in the power of the Holy Spirit, his work of healing and salvation, even among her own members. This is the purpose of the two sacraments of healing: the sacrament of Penance and the sacrament of Anointing of the Sick. (CCC 1421)

Mercy and Sin

There is a beautiful link between God's mercy, the forgiveness of sins, and the Eucharist as the covenant of His blood. "The Gospel is the revelation in Jesus Christ of God's mercy to sinners. The angel announced to Joseph: 'You shall call his name Jesus, for he will save his people from their sins.' The same is true of the Eucharist, the sacrament of redemption: 'This is my blood of the covenant, which is poured out for many for the forgiveness of sins'" (CCC 1846).

The healing that begins in the confessional is sealed in the Eucharist. In a related *Catechism* passage is reference to a physician who probes a wound before treating it. God's Word and Spirit cast light on sin to bring about conversion. This is the amazing work of divine mercy.

As St. Paul affirms, "Where sin increased, grace abounded all the more." But to do its work grace must uncover sin so as to convert our hearts and bestow on us "righteousness to eternal life through Jesus Christ our Lord." Like a physician who probes the wound before treating it, God, by his Word and by his Spirit, casts a living light on sin: Conversion *requires convincing of sin*; it includes the interior judgment of conscience, and this, being a proof of the action of the Spirit of truth in man's inmost being, becomes at the same time the start of a new grant of grace and love: "Receive the Holy Spirit." Thus in this "convincing concerning sin" we discover *a double gift*: the gift of the truth of conscience and the gift of the certainty of redemption. The Spirit of truth is the Consoler. (CCC 1848)

The above text reminds us that the art of forgiveness is the work of the Spirit of God. The Holy Spirit is ever ready to aid us in giving and receiving divine mercy.

Releasing the Poison of Unforgiveness

St. Philip Neri tells us, "If a man finds it very hard to forgive injuries, let him look at a Crucifix, and think that Christ shed all His Blood for him, and not only forgave His enemies, but even prayed His Heavenly Father to forgive them also. Let him remember that when he says the Our Father, every day, instead of asking pardon for his sins, he is calling down vengeance on himself."

Calling down vengeance on myself? Yes! This is the sober truth of the danger of unforgiveness. Failure to forgive routinely tears asunder families, neighborhoods, nations, and the Church. Failure to forgive is a major human problem manifested in the dire daily news. I would propose that the inspired Jubilee Year of Mercy[7] initiated by Pope Francis is God's spotlight on the *world of unforgiveness* so that it may stop escalating to the point of war and destruction. We ardently implore the reign of God's mercy in our hearts, families, friendships, work, Church, nation, and world. Scott Hahn explains the consequences of unforgiveness:

> The love of God does not abide in an unmerciful heart (1 Jn 3:17), and the mercy of God will not penetrate into the human heart if we fail to forgive those who have trespassed against us (Matt 6:14–15) (CCC 1847, 2840). Thus, according to Pope John Paul II, "mercy constitutes the fundamental content of the messianic message of Christt...." His disciples and followers understood and practiced mercy in the same way. Mercy never ceased to reveal itself, in their hearts and in their actions, as an especially creative proof of the love which does not allow itself to be "conquered by evil," but overcomes "evil with good" (cf. Rom 12:21) (*Dives in Misericordia* n. 6).[8]

Releasing the poison of unforgiveness can be a creative process. It requires a new level of trust in God and others. When we are traumatized, betrayed, abandoned, or hurt by others, our ability to trust can be broken. Do we desire our wounds to define us, or do we want to be healed? We can forgive others and ourselves through the sacred wounds of Jesus.

---

[7] The Jubilee Year of Mercy refers to the holy year that Pope Francis declared starting December 8, 2015, through November 20, 2016. He wishes all of humanity to repent, to turn toward Christ, and to receive mercy.

[8] Scott Hahn, *Catholic Bible Dictionary* (New York: Doubleday, 2009), 603.

Unforgiveness Is Costly

Unforgiveness afflicts a person with spiritual darkness and makes him vulnerable to increased spiritual warfare. I see this often in the deliverance ministry, wherein demons try to thwart forgiveness in order to hold the soul captive. Unforgiveness has a negative effect on mental, emotional, and physical health. A general consensus among mental-health professionals is that the common characteristics of unforgiving people include:

+ increased anxiety symptoms

+ increased paranoia

+ increased narcissism

+ increased frequency of psychosomatic complications

+ increased incidence of heart disease

+ less resistance to physical illness

+ increased incidences of both depression and callousness toward others

The common characteristics of forgiving people include:

+ less anxiety and depression

+ better health outcomes

+ a greater ability to cope with stress

+ increased closeness to God and others

Forgiveness does not take us back to where we were before we were hurt. It might be a diversion of two paths, but both can move forward freely. Forgiveness is growth in knowledge and understanding of ourselves and others.

Profile in Mercy: St. Peter

Christ was obviously per-
turbed when He said to Peter, "Get behind me, Satan!
You are a hindrance to me;
for you are not on the side of
God, but of men" (Matt. 16:23). Can you imagine how
Peter felt when Jesus called him Satan? Certainly Peter
is not Satan, but Satan used Peter as a mouthpiece of
demonic temptation when he spoke, "God forbid, Lord!"
in response to Jesus' saying that He "must go to Jerusalem
and suffer many things from the elders and chief priests
and scribes, and be killed, and on the third day be raised"
(Matt. 16:21, 22). Like Peter, *we* sometimes become the
mouthpiece of the deceiver when we speak to another
according to merely human concerns, not God's.

At the Last Supper, Jesus said, "Simon, Simon,
behold, Satan demanded to have you, that he might
sift you like wheat, but I have prayed for you that your
faith may not fail; and when you have turned again,
strengthen your brethren." But Peter replied, "Lord, I
am ready to go with you to prison and to death." Jesus
answered, "I tell you, Peter, the cock will not crow this
day, until you three times deny that you know me"(Luke
22:31–34). Afterward, Peter fell asleep in the Garden of
Olives instead of keeping a prayer vigil as Jesus agonized

and sweat blood. Then Peter denied Jesus three times to save himself. At Calvary Peter ran from the Cross. Peter was Christ's right-hand man. Peter betrayed, disobeyed, and ran away. Did Peter's actions hurt Jesus? Christ had a human heart, experienced human emotions and pain. Yes, the heart of Jesus would have been hurt by the denial of His close friend. Did Christ replace Peter or change His mind about the person to whom He entrusted the leadership of His Church? No. Christ had a perfect plan. Jesus accepted Peter's repentance, affirmed him, and raised him up. Jesus loved Peter and used Peter's weakness to glorify Divine Mercy. Peter was crucified upside down: a martyr of love.

After Peter's transformation at Pentecost, he would never repeat his mistakes. He was able to receive God's forgiveness. He became transformed by Divine Mercy. Jesus gave Peter a second and third chance. We believe in a God of second and third chances. Jesus never gives up on a person.

Personal or Group Spiritual Exercise

The Teaching of the Word of God
Read Luke 23:39–43: The Good Thief

One of the criminals who were hanged railed at him, saying, "Are you not the Christ? Save yourself and us!"

But the other rebuked him, saying, "Do you not fear God, since you are under the same sentence of condemnation? And we indeed justly; for we are receiving the due reward of our deeds; but this man has done nothing wrong." And he said, "Jesus, remember me when you come in your kingly power." And he said to him, "Truly, I say to you, today you will be with me in Paradise."

QUESTIONS FOR GROUP OR PERSONAL REFLECTION

1. How does God's mercy for the repentant thief speak to your heart?

2. Think of a time when you received mercy instead of condemnation. What lesson did you learn about God, yourself, or others?

3. Think of a time when you had great difficulty in forgiving yourself or someone else. Can you identify the root cause of the unforgiveness?

4. Consider your three biggest disappointments or mistakes. Offer them up to God's mercy. Say a prayer to let go.

5. Ask Jesus to release *any poison of unforgiveness* from you. Be a vessel of mercy; pray for those who hurt you.

Applying God's Mercy

God's Letter to You

Be not afraid of your Savior, O sinful soul. I make the first move to come to you, for I know that by yourself you are unable to give yourself to me. Child, do not run away from your Father; be willing to talk openly with your God of mercy who wants to speak words of pardon and lavish his graces on you. How dear your soul is to me! I have inscribed your name upon my hand; you are engraved as a deep wound in my Heart.

My child, do you fear the God of mercy? My holiness does not prevent me from being merciful. Behold, for you I have established a throne of mercy on earth—the tabernacle—and from this throne I desire to enter into your heart. I am not surrounded by a retinue or guards. You can come to me at any moment, at any time; I want to speak to you, and I desire to grant you grace.[9]

Your Letter to God

---

[9] *God Who Is Rich in Mercy: Meditations and Prayers to the Divine Mercy* (Kraków: Shrine of Divine Mercy, 2000), 63–65.

2

RAYS OF DIVINE MERCY
ON THE FAMILY

Healing from
Fear to Trust

Christ is full of tender mercy for families. That Jesus Christ was
born of a woman, the Virgin Mary, and entered into a family,
where He remained for thirty years in Nazareth, is the unmistak-
able sign of God's love for the family. During His public ministry
Jesus entered into the lives of many families. His first miracle
at Cana was on behalf of the family (John 2:1–11). He healed
Peter's mother-in-law (Matt. 8:14–15). He brought Lazarus
back from the dead at the request of his family (John 11:1–44).

IN THIS CHAPTER

+ We will reflect on God's healing mercy that intervenes for the family.

+ We will consider the healing power of trust versus fear.

+ We will learn how to release prayer power into the family for healing.

Christ honored the request of the father with a demonized son and healed him (Mark 9:14–29). Jesus brought a girl back from the dead at the behest of her parents (Luke 8:40–42, 49–56). God in His divine mercy is concerned with the flourishing of families. The rays of merciful love flow upon the family, affirming, healing, and strengthening.

Usually it is in the context of the family that we learn to make a sincere gift of ourselves to another; to serve as Jesus and Mary came to serve and not to be served. Families are called to holiness, but they have a very human side. We love imperfectly and can hurt one another because we live together. We are vulnerable to an unkind word or action. Most of us cherish our families despite the flaws. Since most people pass through a family, we are formed for the better or the worse by it. Here is where divine mercy intervenes for families.

Families are wise to be protective of the holy gift entrusted to them by God — the domestic church. These words have a depth of meaning and they remind us that the family is a community of persons: one man and one woman and their children. So vital is this community of persons that Pope John

Paul II expressed, "The future of humanity passes by way of the family."[10] Family is God's gift to us, to the world. In today's climate of cultural immorality, many families are unraveling and others exist in fear: parents fear for their children; spouses fear for one another. How do we begin to trust God and one another, as we should?

Healing from Fear to Trust

Fear is listed in the *Catechism* under the category of the morality of the passions. Fear is a human passion. Passions are neutral, "neither good nor evil" (CCC 1767). There are many passions, but the principal ones are "love and hatred, desire and fear, joy, sadness, and anger" (CCC 1772). "Emotions and feelings can be taken up *into the virtues* or *perverted by the vices*" (CCC 1769). Our fear trigger can be used for good or for evil. God, in His mercy, asks us to trust in Him so that our fears are "brought into the virtues" rather than allowing our fear to be "perverted by the vices." For example, when something triggers fear in me, and I turn immediately to God and pray, "Jesus, I trust in You," I am allowing God the opportunity to transform my fear into the virtue of faith. This also prevents the devil from perverting my fear into vice. Habitually giving in to fear undermines faith, hope, and love and negatively impacts our relationships.

What do you want Jesus to do for your family? Ideally, we desire that God sanctify and protect the family. During my international retreats, and on my weekly *Living Eucharist* radio program,

---

[10] Pope John Paul II, *Familiaris Consortio*, November 22, 1981, no. 86, http://w2.vatican.va/.

people confide their prayer intentions. Many are fearful, and this is understandable because of the problems that besiege families. We are carrying heavy burdens for marriages and for our children. Far from despairing, we have a reason and a right to rejoice that we are called to stand for Christ in such a time as this. We have an opportunity for heroic faith, hope, and love.

Irrational fear drains the abundant life from us—the vibrancy that Jesus desires to give His disciples. In prayer we can hear Jesus whispering, "Never give up on hope, never doubt, never tire, never become discouraged, and never fear. Trust, I am with you." He fills the Gospels with such words that should sink into the depths of our hearts.

What Is True Healing?

Catholic healing is, in a word, *resurrection*. Recall the scene: "[H]e cried with a loud voice, 'Lazarus, come out!'" (John 11:43). Christ enters to heal what is dead, broken, sleeping, wounded, disordered, or sick, physically and spiritually. Another word for healing is *redemption*. Christ redeems our sin-sickness and the wounds that result. Reflecting on the Gospels, we see that Jesus healed many people physically, but what should not be forgotten is that sometimes He first forgave the person's sins before healing the physical infirmity, showing that being well spiritually is the priority.

During the fifteen years I worked in the medical field, there were many very sick patients who were some of the most healed people I ever met. For example, I have two friends who are in wheelchairs, Renee and Mary Ann. Renee has been a quadriplegic since the day she broke her neck right before her wedding.

Mary Ann contracted a disease that confined her to a wheelchair. These mothers and wives radiate joy, peace, sage wisdom, and palpable sanctity. They suffer daily and certainly would welcome God's healing. We pray for this, but they remain in wheelchairs, praising God in all things. Christ's healing mercy enfolds them—in their wheelchairs. Renee, an acclaimed Catholic singer, wrote these lyrics: "What if trials of this life are God's mercies in disguise? What if Your healing comes through tears? What if a thousand sleepless nights are what it takes to know You are near?" Can we consider "surrender" a type of healing also?

At the miraculous Marian shrine of Lourdes, not all are healed physically, but every pilgrim receives a touch of healing mercy. I've witnessed amazing miracles at Eucharistic healing services, especially in poorer countries. We ask in faith. We believe in hope. We wait. We accept in trust. God expects us to ask for the healing we need. We can never go wrong to pray for healing with the understanding that God will heal in His surprising way and perfect time.

A diocesan priest friend, Father Sy Nguyen, experienced a miraculous healing recently. Father was in a very serious motorcycle accident and spent months in the hospital undergoing fourteen surgical procedures. His right leg suffered critical injuries. Two ulcers developed, and the wounds would not heal. The wounds became so problematic that his doctor considered the real possibility of soon having to amputate his leg. A parishioner had just returned from the Oratory of St. Joseph in Montreal, Canada, who gave him a vial of the oil from there. Father prayed for healing through the intercession of St. André Bessette and poured the oil directly onto the open wounds. The next day, the oozing ulcers dried up, and Father Nguyen's leg began to heal and was saved. To thank the Lord and St. André Bessette for his miracle, he led a pilgrimage of thanksgiving and honor to the miraculous shrine of the saint last summer.

Mercy is manifested in the asking, waiting, receiving, and accepting of God's way of healing.

Jesus the Divine Physician

The Church looks to Jesus Christ as the Divine Physician, healer of the entire person. The *Catechism* affirms that Christ heals and has given the Church the command to continue His healing ministry. God's mercy is released through the sacraments as the medicine of grace active in the healing process.

> "Heal the sick!" The Church has received this charge from the Lord and strives to carry it out by taking care of the sick as well as by accompanying them with her prayer of intercession. She believes in the life-giving presence of *Christ, the physician of souls and bodies.* This presence is particularly active through the sacraments, and in an altogether special way through the Eucharist, the bread that gives eternal life and that St. Paul suggests is connected with bodily health. (CCC 1421, 1509; emphasis added)

Releasing Prayer Power for the Family

Where does the *power* of prayer come from? The power of Christian prayer derives from a covenant relationship between God and man in Christ. It is the action of God and of man springing forth from the Holy Spirit (cf. CCC 2564). According to Scripture, it is the heart that prays.

It is not surprising that St. John Paul II encouraged families to pray and not to be afraid of risks.

How indispensable is the witness of all families who live their vocation day-by-day; how urgent it is *for families to pray* and for that prayer to increase and to spread throughout the world.... *Do not be afraid* of the risks! God's strength is always far more powerful than your difficulties![11]

Love is risky. Family is risky. Family is at the heart of the great drama of salvation. St. John Paul II urged increasing prayer *within and for* families to strengthen them against the imposing cultural antifamily mentality. Family prayer changes the atmosphere in the home and protects the family by keeping it in close relationship with Christ. Family prayer should be practical, simple, and beautiful.

Peter Kreeft helps us to understand the healing power of prayer in his catechesis on *Jesus:* the shortest, simplest, and *most powerful prayer* in the world:

"The kingdom of God does not consist in talk but in power," says Saint Paul (1 Cor 4:20). The reason this prayer is so powerful is that the name of Jesus is not just a set of letters or sounds. It is not a passive word but a creative word, like the word by which God created the universe. (He *is* the Word by which God created the universe!) Every time we receive Christ in the Eucharist, we are instructed by the liturgy to pray, "Lord, I am not

---

[11] Pope John Paul II, *Letter to Families* (Manchester, NH: Sophia Institute Press, 2014), 10, 95.

worthy that you should enter under my roof, *but only say the word* and my soul shall be healed." All our energy and effort is not strong enough to heal our own souls, but God's word of power is. That word is so powerful that by it God made the universe out of nothing, and by it he is doing the even greater deed of making saints out of sinners. That word is Jesus Christ."[12]

The *Catechism* echoes this teaching: "The invocation of the holy name of Jesus is the simplest way of praying always.... This prayer is possible 'at all times' because it is not one occupation among others but the only occupation: that of loving God, which animates and transfigures every action in Christ Jesus" (CCC 2668).

The prayer that Jesus taught St. Faustina, "Jesus, I trust in You,"[13] testifies to the primacy of trust over fear. Christ has given us a weapon against fear—the simple but profound prayer "Jesus, I trust in You" heals the soul and strengthens the heart.

Many fears need to be healed: fear of fear, fear of the unknown, fear of failure, fear of rejection or abandonment, fear of the past or the future, fear of death or life—the list continues. What is God's remedy? "[L]ove casts out fear" (1 John 4:18). Prayers of trust are highly effective weapons. "[F]ear not, for I am with you, be not dismayed, for I am your God; I will strengthen you, I will help you, I will uphold you with my victorious right hand" (Isa. 41:10).

---

[12] Peter Kreeft, "'Jesus': The Shortest, Simplest, and Most Powerful Prayer in the World," in *Prayer for Beginners* (San Francisco: Ignatius Press, 2000), chap. 9; posted on Peter Kreeft's website, accessed June 13, 2015, http://www.peterkreeft.com/topics-more/jesus-prayer.htm.

[13] St. Faustina, *Diary*, no. 327.

Mercy for the Soul of the Family

The transformation of our families begins with my personal conversion so that I radiate the merciful love of Jesus. True conjugal and familial love is fire tested. Is there a willingness to sacrifice, serve, and self-empty for the sake of a greater love that is priceless, permanent, and perfect? There is a love that casts out fear. There is a love that is noble, beautiful, and dynamic. It does not count the cost. It just loves selflessly. This is the love that God wants to cultivate within our families. This is the way of love that Paul eloquently writes about in his letter to the Corinthians (cf. 1 Cor. 13:1–13).

In today's battle for the soul of marriage and family, trust is necessary. Jesus told St. Faustina: "The graces of My mercy are drawn by means of one vessel only, and that is trust. The more a soul trusts, the more it will receive. Souls that trust boundlessly are a great comfort to Me.... I pour out all the treasures of My graces upon them."[14] Trust is life giving and empowers us to step out in faith to do the greater works of mercy.

In retreat work I joyfully witness God's healing mercy. Once a woman struggled about her self-worth because her mother said something derogatory to her when she was a teenager. On the retreat she recalled the hurtful words that haunted her for thirty years. I encouraged her to ask the Holy Spirit for insight into the true intent of her mother in the context of the hurtful words. She then brought the painful memory to the Blessed Sacrament during the retreat. The Lord graciously gave her deep insights as to how her mother was raised and why she expressed herself in the manner that hurt her daughter. Armed with that knowledge,

---

[14] Ibid., no. 1578.

the woman was able to let go of the false perception of herself and accept her mother with more compassion. She began to trust God, herself, and her mother. Healing can begin with just a small step.

Profile in Mercy: Author's Story: Forgiving the Murderers

When my husband and I arrived at St. Mary's Hospital emergency room, nothing could have prepared us for the trauma we were about to experience. Lying on a hospital gurney was my husband's beloved father, who had suffered blunt-force trauma to his head and upper body. He was beaten beyond recognition. He had been found lying in a pool of blood on the sidewalk in front of his lumber business.

Attempting to save his life, doctors ordered a frontal lobectomy (brain surgery). In shock, we prayed and hoped. After a few hours, the surgeon reported that he would not survive. However, he could live a few hours more on life support so family could be gathered. At a father's bedside, a German-Irish family said goodbye to a strong, joyful, wise husband, dad, and grandfather. I recall listening to his final breaths, slow and labored. Then one final gasp, and his breathing stopped. He was no longer with us. I had faith that his particular judgment[1] would go well. While our faith supported us, the violence of his death caused excruciating pain and trauma.

Police surmised that robbers assaulted him with a large timber as he entered the business office alone on a Saturday morning. This murder case aired on the television program *America's Most Wanted*, but to this day the case is unsolved.

The church was filled on the day of the funeral, and everyone was mystified by the horror of his violent death. During the funeral the Lord reminded me, "This is the fruit of a culture of death. The violence of abortion breeds more violence."

That night, my husband decided that we should not talk about this anymore; we should move forward to care for his mother and the family business. That is what the family tried to do, but nothing would ever be the same.

I could not easily move forward after such violent trauma. I felt vulnerable to more violence and murder; nothing felt safe. Fear and anger overcame me. In private, I wept often. I began praying before the Blessed Sacrament for long hours, conversing with Jesus. I expressed anger, "Where were You, Lord? How could You allow this?" I was praying for justice.

After a few weeks, the Lord spoke to my heart: "I want you to pray for the murderers please." I protested and refused to do so. I remained very unsettled. Each day before the

---

[1] The Catholic doctrine of the particular judgment is that, immediately after death, the eternal destiny of each separated soul is decided by the just judgment of God.

Blessed Sacrament, Jesus spoke to my heart: "I am inviting you to echo my words from the Cross: 'Father, forgive them, for they know not what they are doing.'" I told the Lord that I would say those words but not mean them. Over time, He kept prompting me to repeat His words of forgiveness.

When I finally prayed, in earnest, for the salvation of the souls of the murderers, my peace and joy returned. I was set free. I surrendered justice to God and genuinely hoped that the murderers would not be eternally lost. When I prayed for the murderers' salvation, Jesus flooded my soul with deep awareness of His unfathomable mercy for sinners. I understood that *no one*, even the greatest sinner, is outside God's mercy.

Personal or Group Spiritual Exercise

The Teaching of the Word of God
Read: Luke 15:11–32: The Parable of the Prodigal Son.

There was a man who had two sons; and the younger of them said to his father, "Father, give me the share of property that falls to me." And he divided his living between them. Not many days later, the younger son gathered all he had and took his journey into a far country, and there he squandered his property in loose living. And when he had spent everything, a great famine arose in that country, and he began to be in want. So he went and joined himself to one of the citizens of that country, who sent him into his fields to feed swine. And he would gladly have fed on the pods that the swine ate; and no one gave him anything. But when he came to himself he said, "How many of my father's hired servants have bread enough and to spare, but I perish here with hunger! I will arise and go to my father, and I will say to him, 'Father, I have sinned against heaven and before you; I am no longer worthy to be called your son; treat me as one of your hired servants.'" And he arose and came to his father. But while he was yet at a distance, his father saw him and had compassion, and ran and embraced him and kissed him. And the son said to him, "Father, I have sinned against heaven and before you; I am no longer worthy to be called your son." But the father said to his servants, "Bring quickly the best robe, and put it on him; and put a ring on his hand, and shoes on his feet; and bring the fatted calf and kill it, and let us eat and make merry; for this my son was dead, and is alive again; he was lost, and is found." And they began to make merry.

Now his elder son was in the field; and as he came and drew near to the house, he heard music and dancing. And he called one of the servants and asked what this meant. And he said to him, "Your brother has come, and your father has killed the fatted calf, because he has received him safe and sound." But he was angry and refused to go in. His father came out and entreated him, but he answered his father, "Behold, these many years I have served you, and I never disobeyed your command; yet you never gave me a kid, that I might make merry with my friends. But when this son of yours came, who has devoured your living with harlots, you killed for him the fatted calf!" And he said to him, "Son, you are always with me, and all that is mine is yours. It was fitting to make merry and be glad, for this your brother was dead, and is alive; he was lost, and is found."

QUESTIONS FOR GROUP OR PERSONAL REFLECTION

1. Were you ever a prodigal child? What did you learn about yourself, God, and others?

2. Has anyone ever been for you the merciful father who welcomed you back with open arms?

3. Reflect on the reaction of the older faithful brother. Have you ever been resentful or self-righteous in the face of merciful love for someone else?

4. Reflect on your family and how you were brought up. Did fear or unforgiveness impact your family? Bring any wounds to God for healing.

5. Reflect on a time when you were *very* afraid. How did God bring you through the fear?

Applying God's Mercy

God's Letter to You

Tell souls where they are to look for solace; that is, in the Tribunal of Mercy [the Sacrament of Reconciliation]. There the greatest miracles take place (and) are incessantly repeated. To avail oneself of this miracle, it is not necessary to go on a great pilgrimage or to carry out some external ceremony: it suffices to come with faith to the feet of My representative and to reveal to him one's misery, and the miracle of Divine Mercy will be fully demonstrated. Were a soul like a decaying corpse so that from a human standpoint, there would be no (hope of) restoration and everything would already be lost, it is not so with God. The miracle of Divine Mercy restores the soul in full.[15]

Your Letter to God

---

[15] St. Faustina, *Diary*, no. 1448.

3

RAYS OF DIVINE MERCY ON THE POOR, THE SICK, AND THE SUFFERING

Healing from Shame to Mercy

*Suffering exists in the world in order to
release love, in order to give birth to works of love
towards neighbor, in order to transform the whole
of human civilization into a "civilization of love." In
this love the salvific meaning of suffering is completely
accomplished and reaches its definitive dimension.*

—John Paul II, *Apostolic Letter on the
Christian Meaning of Human Suffering*

St. John Paul II's words in the opening quotation are especially poignant because he bore witness to the Christian meaning of suffering. The Polish saint showed the world the face of the Suffering Servant, Jesus, whom we long to see and touch. Suffering found him, and he did not recoil. He let the whole world look upon his physical diminishment so that we may see the triumph of love, the glory of God flowing from a pierced heart of mercy.

IN THIS CHAPTER

+ We will reflect on the Christian meaning of human suffering.

+ We will seek God's mercy to heal shame, the ache of the soul.

+ We will consider God's merciful love for the poor, the sick, and the suffering so that we may become vessels of mercy and healing.

There was a profound and unforgettable moment captured on global public television when Pope John Paul II could no longer speak although he tried repeatedly. The voice of the Good Shepherd was muted so we could learn that love speaks more perfectly in the silent witness of suffering souls. Only in heaven will we know the number of souls St. John Paul II carried to God by the *love* with which he carried the cross. A generation was given two amazing witnesses of God's merciful love for the poor, the sick, and the suffering: St. John Paul II and Blessed Mother Teresa.

I would propose that Mary, Mother of Divine Mercy, carried her devoted priest-son who became Christ's vicar as he carried the Cross of Jesus for the Church. The seven-times pierced heart of the Mother of Mercy embraces whoever suffers in union with her Son, Jesus. So perfect a Mother could do no less for God's family entrusted to her solicitude. It was her courageous love that planted her feet firmly at the foot of the Cross. On Calvary she was valiant, believing, and fully engaged in the sacrifice of her Son according to the Father's will. Mary is no stranger to suffering. The Passion of her Son resonated in every atom of her being. The Mother of

Mercy is a friend to all who suffer and are in need of courage. It was Mary's trust in God at the moment of the Annunciation that gave the world the Divine Mercy. Trust in God releases healing mercy.

Divine Mercy Transforms Suffering

Life on earth includes suffering, and every person experiences some form of it. Suffering has a way of finding us, no matter how much we try to avoid it. One might suffer from physical or mental illness, the infirmity of old age, the frustration of a difficult work situation, daily responsibilities under emotional pain, or the sadness of some loss (privations, accidents, abandonment, traumas). Suffering is a spiritual mystery not to be solved, or simply endured, but to be entered into as a passage with purpose. In the light of faith, suffering can become a school of love in which we learn priceless lessons about God's inexhaustible mercy, about human resiliency, and about the beauty of selfless love.

Thirty years ago my first priest spiritual director gave me the gift of Pope John Paul II's apostolic letter *Salvifici Doloris* (*Salvific Suffering*). Actually he gifted it to my husband, who, while suffering from back surgery, was not too enthused to be reading about suffering. The subtitle *On the Christian Meaning of Human Suffering* intrigued me, although I had suffered little in my life up to that point. I read this papal letter with amazement. The radical truth of coredeeming suffering: the daring challenge resonated in my heart as a spiritual work that is altogether transcendent and beautiful. It reoriented my thinking about embracing the Cross of Jesus in my life. Admittedly it is easier to read about suffering than it is to experience it. Suffering would find me later, and then, I drew strength from St. John Paul II's teaching.

At the risk of being overly simplistic, after reading the truth about the Christian meaning of suffering, I recalled the often-spoken words of my parents to their five children, "Offer it up! Quick! Offer it up to God!" As a child, I was consoled by this idea. As an adult, in times of suffering, I find consolation by placing my suffering in Christ's Passion. His sorrowful mysteries make my suffering seem like a teardrop in the crimson ocean of divine mercy. His Passion heals my self-pity.

Christ Enters the World of Suffering

Why does God allow so much suffering to touch the human family? This is the universal question. God not only permits suffering in the world, but He preached that we would *definitely* suffer as He did. Jesus was not a politically correct preacher, nor did He attempt to soften the truth: "And he said to all, 'If any man would come after me, let him deny himself and take up his cross daily and follow me'" (Luke 9:23). The gospel is demanding because God makes a provision to live the demands by the power of His love poured into our hearts at Baptism.

We do not carry the cross or suffer life's trials on our own power. It is written, "Not by might, nor by power, but by my Spirit, says the LORD of hosts" (Zech. 4:6). The Holy Spirit empowers us to carry our cross. Suffering teaches us the art of accompaniment on the journey. Jesus accepted the help of Simon of Cyrene on the road to Calvary.

Christ entered into our world of suffering and took the pain upon Himself. He became sin and death so that we may live forever in the embrace of divine mercy—Paradise. Jesus is the revelation of the suffering servant's dignity and mission. The saints, by their example of red or white martyrdom of love,[16] compel us to trust in God's mercy. God made us capable of great sorrow and joy, and often joy and sorrow intertwine. Catholicism will continue to call forth witnesses and martyrs.

In *Salvifici Doloris* the pope writes, "What is evil? This question seems, in a certain sense, inseparable from the theme of suffering."[17] Since I will write on the theme of evil and spiritual warfare in another chapter, I will not expound on it here. I bring it up to assure readers that the above texts are not intended to glamorize suffering for its own sake. Suffering is an evil in the world, according to Christian teaching. Suffering was not in God's original design in the Garden of Eden. It is the result of sin.

Author Robert G. Schroeder offers a helpful analogy, "The presence of evil in the world is kind of like the holes in a piece of Swiss cheese. It is a negative reality that takes away from the good and whole order of God's creation."[18] Christianity assures us that "in everything God works for good" (Rom. 8:28)—turning

---

[16] Red martyrdom refers to being killed for the Faith. White martyrdom, Fr. John Hardon tells us, "means living a life of witness to the Catholic faith under constant duress and psychological pressure from a world that rejects Christ's followers even as it rejected the Incarnate Son of God when He came into the world in first century Palestine." Fr. John Hardon, S.J., "Questions and Answers," "Father John A. Hardon, S.J., Archives," The Real Presence Association, accessed August 19, 2015, http://www.therealpresence.org/archives/Q_and_A/Q_and_A_001. htm.

[17] John Paul II, *Salvifici Doloris* (Boston: Pauline Books, 1984), 2.7.

[18] Robert G. Schroeder, *John Paul II and the Meaning of Suffering* (Huntington, IN: Our Sunday Visitor, 2008), 27.

the negative into the positive. Divine mercy fills the holes caused by evil with the wholeness of love.

Transforming Shame to Merciful Love

In his general audience on May 28, 1980, John Paul II explained the concupiscence[19] and shame that resulted from the fall and original sin: "The words in Genesis 3:10, 'I was afraid, because I was naked, and I hid myself,' provide evidence of man's first experience of shame before his Creator — a shame that could also be called 'cosmic'. It is the shame produced in humanity itself." In practical terms, shame includes feeling unworthy, unlovable, inadequate, sinful, dirty, and burdened by past sins and failures.

The prophet Jeremiah records one type of shame in reference to Israel's rebellion and God's wrath: " 'They have healed the wound of my people lightly, saying, "Peace, peace," when there is no peace. Were they ashamed when they committed abomination? No, they were not at all ashamed; they did not know how to blush. Therefore they shall fall among those who fall; at the time that I punish them, they shall be overthrown,' says the Lord" (Jer. 6:14–15).

We should blush because of our sins against God and others. The world tries to erase appropriate shame. Shame, guilt, and condemnation are related to sin but in different ways. Shame is deeper than guilt and is not based on some wrong that we

---

[19] "Concupiscence: Insubordination of man's desires to the dictates of reason, and the propensity of human nature to sin as a result of original sin and unruly desires of the will, such as pride, ambition, and envy." Hardon, *Modern Catholic Dictionary*, s.v. "concupiscence."

did. Rather, the center of the soul aches of *being* wrong. Shame touches the nerve of self in a painful way; more piercing than condemnation is the feeling of shame. With shame we feel the depths of our depravity and long for healing.

Scripture makes cases for and against shame. For example, a case against shame is found in Isaiah 54:4: "Fear not, for you will not be ashamed; be not confounded, for you will not be put to shame; for you will forget the shame of your youth." A case for shame is found in 1 Corinthians 15:34: "Come to your right mind, and sin no more. For some have no knowledge of God. I say this to your shame."

The Lord can use either type of shame for our sanctification. Whether we blush when we look closely at our sin or turn away, refusing to blush for our offenses against God and man, divine mercy is a healing prescription. God's love convicts the soul of sin, and God's mercy forgives the repentant sinner. God's mercy keeps pricking the conscience, piercing it with the pain of its sin. When we confess and repent, God's mercy cures the wound with the balm of forgiveness.

We have an opponent of divine mercy named the Accuser who exerts spiritual oppression to hold a person captive to sin, condemnation, and shame. Our human weakness can also lead us to places of guilt and shame, especially when we are in need of spiritual healing. The embrace of the Father heals the prodigal children who turn around with repentance and conversion, seeking to come back home.

God never departs from sinners. The healing rays of divine mercy draw us to return to our senses, to be reconciled. Divine mercy transforms shame into humble gratitude. Paul assures us, "Therefore, if any one is in Christ, he is a new creation; the old has passed away, behold, the new has come" (2 Cor.

5:17). Like Lazarus, Jesus calls us out of the tomb to take off the death wraps.

Profile in Mercy: Blessed Mother Teresa

Mother Teresa radiated the mercy of Christ for the poor, the sick, and the suffering souls she cared for in the streets of Calcutta. A friend of mine who accompanied Mother Teresa in Calcutta was a woman of means who had never been up close to the immensity of suffering that she saw in the streets of that city. When she and Mother arrived, my friend was overwhelmed emotionally by the scope of the poverty, the sickness, and the suffering. She spontaneously burst into tears and could not stop crying. She sensed that Mother was somewhat perturbed at her reaction to the poor people, but Mother did not say anything at first.

On the second day, however, when Mother saw more tears streaming down my friend's face as they walked the streets of Calcutta among the poor, she spoke firmly: "These suffering people do not need your tears; they are in dire need of your smile." Abruptly, her tears ceased, and, observing Mother Teresa ministering to the poor, she began to imitate her genuine smile.

Mother Teresa stopped to pick up a dying man in her arms to comfort him. Her smile was radiant with joy as she held the man's head and stroked his face and arms. The woman overheard Mother assuring the man as she smiled lovingly upon him, "Soon you will meet *my* God." She noted that Mother did not try to convert the dying man to *her* God. However, the Holy Spirit was at work. The dying man replied, "If your God makes you *so joyful,* then I want to meet your God." Mother continued to smile as the man expired in her arms. Hopefully, he soon met her God.

This story exemplifies God's preferential love for poor, suffering souls. The Lord aims the rays of divine mercy upon them. People who are spiritually or materially impoverished are in need of signs of hope—like what Peter, James and John experienced on Mount Tabor at the moment of Christ's Transfiguration. We can give the poor, the sick, and the suffering a glimpse of divine light when we reach out to them. Mother Teresa, the *saint of the smile* for the poor, the sick, and the dying, revealed the secret of God's mercy in the simplicity of a radiant smile for those who suffer. Mother emptied herself to become poor like the people entrusted to her by God. The rays of mercy flowed freely through her unencumbered heart. Isn't it beautiful that something as simple as a loving smile for a suffering person can become a work of mercy? For authenticity, our smile must be born of the realization that our God has been merciful to us.

Personal or Group Spiritual Exercise

The Teaching of the Word of God
Read Luke 16:19–31: The Rich Man and Lazarus.

"There was a rich man, who was clothed in purple and fine linen and who feasted sumptuously every day. And at his gate lay a poor man named Lazarus, full of sores, who desired to be fed with what fell from the rich man's table; moreover the dogs came and licked his sores.

"The poor man died and was carried by the angels to Abraham's bosom. The rich man also died and was buried; and in Hades, being in torment, he lifted up his eyes, and saw Abraham far off and Lazarus in his bosom. And he called out, 'Father Abraham, have mercy upon me, and send Lazarus to dip the end of his finger in water and cool my tongue; for I am in anguish in this flame.' But Abraham said, 'Son, remember that you in your lifetime received your good things, and Lazarus in like manner evil things; but now he is comforted here, and you are in anguish. And besides all this, between us and you a great chasm has been fixed, in order that those who would pass from here to you may not be able, and none may cross from there to us.' And he said, 'Then I beg you, father, to send him to my father's house, for I have five brothers, so that he may warn them, lest they also come into this place of torment.' But Abraham said, 'They have Moses and the prophets; let them hear them.' And he said, 'No, father Abraham; but if some one goes to them from the dead, they will repent.' He said to him, 'If they do not hear Moses and the prophets, neither will they be convinced if some one should rise from the dead.' "

QUESTIONS FOR GROUP OR PERSONAL REFLECTION

1. Like the rich man, have you ever been indifferent to someone suffering in your midst? If so, can you identify the root cause of your indifference?

2. Was there a time when you could relate to the poor man at Lazarus's door? If so, how did God uphold you?

3. When you have experienced suffering (physical, emotional, spiritual, financial), what did you learn about yourself, God, and others?

4. Reflecting on the story of Mother Teresa, how can you put mercy into action for the poor, the sick, the suffering, or the dying?

5. In light of the cosmic shame that began with Adam and Eve (Gen. 3:10: "I was afraid, because I was naked, and I hid myself"), is your self-image in need of healing?

Applying God's Mercy

God's Letter to You
Poor soul, I see that you suffer much and that you do not have even the strength to converse with Me. So I will speak to you. Even though your sufferings were very great, do not lose heart or give in to despondency. But tell Me, my child, who has dared to wound

your heart? Tell Me everything, be sincere in dealing with Me, and reveal all the wounds of your heart. I will heal them, and your suffering will become a source of your sanctification. My child, do not be discouraged. Let us talk in detail about everything that weighs so heavily upon your heart. Talk to Me simply, as a friend to a friend. Tell Me now, My child, what hinders you from advancing in holiness? It is because you are not of this world that the world hates you. First it persecuted Me. Persecution is a sign that you are following in My footsteps faithfully. I realize how painful it is not to be understood, and especially by those whom one loves and with whom one has been very open. But suffice it to know that I understand all your troubles and misery. So approach this fountain of mercy often, to draw with the vessel of trust whatever you need.[20]

---

[20] St. Faustina, *Diary*, no. 1487.

Your Letter to God

4

RAYS OF DIVINE MERCY ON
FRIENDS AND ENEMIES

Healing from Anxiety to Peace

But I say to you, Love your enemies and pray for those who
persecute you, so that you may be sons of your Father who is in
heaven; for he makes his sun rise on the evil and on the good, and
sends rain on the just and on the unjust.

—Matthew 5:43–45

Peace of soul is the tranquility of order: an ordered heart, an
ordered life according to God's precepts. Christ says, "Peace I
leave with you; my peace I give to you; not as the world gives do
I give to you. Let not your hearts be troubled, neither let them
be afraid" (John 14:27). What is this peace that Jesus gives? The
psalmist gives us a clue, "He who dwells in the shelter of the Most
High, who abides in the shadow of the Almighty, will say to the
Lord, 'My refuge and my fortress; my God, in whom I trust.' For
he will deliver you from the snare of the fowler" (Ps. 91:1–3).
Dwelling in the shelter of the Most High is peace that surpasses
all understanding.

IN THIS CHAPTER

+ We will consider that God's mercy redeems anxiety and gives peace.

+ We will reflect on how to shine rays of mercy on our enemies.

+ We will reflect on how to shine rays of mercy on our friends.

Among other things, the shelter of the Almighty includes the Barque of Peter: Christ's Church. In this great ship we ride the river of grace, anchored in the truth, able to live in the peace that only Jesus gives. Christ, our Captain, is with us.

Times of stillness (prayer) in the embrace of His peace strengthen us for the times when storms arise and we think that Jesus is asleep in our sinking boat. He tells us, "Let not your hearts be troubled" because He is with us as He was with David against Goliath. He knows our spiritual enemies are many; the world is full of snares; our flesh is weak even though our spirits are willing. He assures, "I will rescue you from the snare of the fowler." Remember how often He has rescued you. Sometimes, at the very last moment, He does something amazing. He absorbs our anxiety and gives us His peace, which the world cannot give.

Divine Mercy Redeems Anxiety

Christ famously said, "Martha, Martha, you are anxious and troubled about many things; one thing is needful. Mary has chosen the good portion, which shall not be taken away from her" (Luke 10:41–42).

For our reflection we want to consider that the Lord is not *admonishing* Martha as much as He is *inviting* her to choose the better portion of allowing Jesus to transform her anxiousness about many things into the peace that Mary finds by sitting at the feet of the Master and *listening* to Him. More could be said, but for our purpose we make the one point of how Christ transforms human anxiety. The anxiety of humanity in the Old Testament is completely transformed in the New Testament because of the redeeming Cross of Jesus.

According to the National Institute of Mental Health:

> Anxiety is a normal reaction to stress and can actually be beneficial in some situations. For some people, however, anxiety can become excessive, and while the person suffering may realize it is excessive they may also have difficulty controlling it and it may negatively affect their day-to-day living. There are a wide variety of anxiety disorders, including post-traumatic stress disorder, obsessive-compulsive disorder, and specific phobias to name a few. Collectively they are among the most common mental disorders experienced by Americans.[21] An estimated forty million adults over the age of twenty or eighteen percent of Americans are clinically diagnosed with anxiety, of which one third receive treatment.[22]

---

[21] "Any Anxiety Disorder among Adults," National Institutes of Health, accessed June 14, 2015, http://www.nimh.nih.gov/health/statistics/prevalence/any-anxiety-disorder-among-adults.shtml.

[22] Ibid.

An important distinction about *Christian anxiety* is made in Hans Urs von Balthasar's book *The Christian and Anxiety*:

> Christianity is intent upon and capable of delivering man from sin-anxiety, provided that he opens himself up to that redemption and its conditions. In the place of sin-anxiety, it provides him with anxiety-free access to God in faith, love, and hope—which, however, because they stem from the Cross, can in and of themselves put forth a new, grace-filled form of anxiety that stems from Catholic solidarity and shares in Christ's work of atonement....
>
> Insofar as we are sinners ... the anxiety of sin is not simply taken away from us by the objective act of redemption on the Cross but rather is set before us even in the New Testament. We are permitted to leave sin-anxiety behind us to the degree that we appropriate in truth the living faith offered to us from the Cross, that is, a faith active in our lives.[23]

Trust in God Is Living Faith

Trust in God is faith that is alive and active in daily life. We thank the Lord for redeeming our anxiety. When anxiety arises, we hand it over to Christ. He takes it upon Himself and gives us His priceless peace.

Jesus has steadied me at the most anxious moments of my life: after the murder of my father-in-law; at the scene of the

---

[23] Hans Urs von Balthasar, *The Christian and Anxiety* (San Francisco: Ignatius Press, 2000), 96, 106.

accident where our high school son's car was found upside down at the bottom of a ravine with him and two friends inside; during our grade school son's hospitalization for weeks due to spinal meningitis; during the four times when my mother nearly died. Christ took my anxiety and gave me His peace. I must be willing to surrender my anxiety to Jesus.

Rays of Mercy on Enemies

During His Crucifixion, with dying breath, Christ spoke the essential word of divine mercy, "Father, forgive them; for they know not what they do" (Luke 23:34). Jesus Christ forgave those who, with inhuman cruelty, inflicted torturous pain on Him to the point of death. Only in light of Christ's mercy for sinners, for enemies, can we hope to forgive those who hurt us.

Who is my enemy? Many people relate to these words of the psalmist: "For wicked and deceitful mouths are opened against me, speaking against me with lying tongues. They beset me with words of hate, and attack me without cause. In return for my love they accuse me, even as I make prayer for them. So they reward me evil for good, and hatred for my love" (Ps. 109:2–5).

St. Luke writes, "But I say to you that hear, Love your enemies, do good to those who hate you, bless those who curse you, pray for those who abuse you. To him who strikes you on the cheek, offer the other also; and from him who takes away your cloak do not withhold your coat as well. Give to every one who begs from you; and of him who takes away your goods do not ask them again. And as you wish that men would do to you, do so to them" (Luke 6:27–31).

Forgiving family and friends is difficult, but we can usually do so with greater ease because of the love that we have experienced for each other. With family and friends, we have a history of good memories, loving encounters that help us to let go of unforgiveness.

Forgiveness of enemies is also a matter of love; the love I have for Jesus Christ. The Passion, death, and Resurrection of Jesus Christ are one continuous act of divine mercy into which we are drawn at Baptism. In identifying ourselves with Christ, we extend God's mercy to enemies.

A story of forgiveness is given by Mother Teresa: "When the police asked an alcoholic man in one of our homes in Australia, who had been beaten up by another alcoholic man, for the name of the culprit, he refused to give it. When police went away, the Sisters asked him why he did not give the name of the man who had beaten him. He replied, 'His suffering is not going to make my suffering less!' He gave until it hurt. He forgave his brother."[24]

Some might have faced enemies in situations of war that required them to kill their enemies in defense of self, country, or God. The act of mercy then is to pray for the salvation of the souls of the deceased. The accounts of Christian martyrs convey the forgiveness given to their assassins.

There is something indescribably beautiful in the forgiveness we can give to our enemies because it is the essence of Christ-like mercy. The Christ life within us makes us capable of great acts of mercy. We have only to unleash that Christ life within us to be capable of merciful behavior.

---

[24] Missionaries of Charity, *Mother Teresa of Calcutta Official Commemorative Booklet*, prepared on the occasion of the Beatification of Mother Teresa of Calcutta (Rome: 2003).

Rays of Mercy on Friends

As human beings we ardently seek love and understanding; we need to know that we matter, that someone cares. God's provision for this is friendship. Friendship comes in many forms: brother and sister, parent and child, husband and wife, male and female, and any combination of these. "The scene of the Last Supper reveals Christ's great desire to share his supernatural secrets with his friends, for friends are to be one heart and soul. What makes a relationship spiritual is that its very center of gravity is mutual or shared participation in the following of Christ."[25]

The Church's history is rich in spiritual friendships that produced mutual sanctity, including those of Jonathan and David, Mary and Joseph, Jesus and Joseph, Mary Magdalene and Jesus, Augustine and Monica, Benedict and Scholastica, Clare and Francis of Assisi, Catherine of Siena and Raymond of Capua, Teresa of Ávila and John of the Cross, Basil and Gregory, Clare and Agnes of Prague, Jane de Chantal and Francis de Sales, and Rose of Lima and Martin de Porres. Their stories exemplify intimate friendships in Christ. Spiritual friendships are great gifts in life. Cherish and nurture them, especially with prayer.

Of course, not all friendships are classified as spiritual friendships. We have colleagues, acquaintances, classmates, and extended family whose friendships are quite different. Friends have access in degrees to our heart. Some friends draw the best out of us, and others, the worst. Like love, friendship is risky but worth it, because friendships enrich our lives.

When a close friend betrays us, it is extremely painful. Some of the worst misunderstandings can occur between the best of

---

[25] Ronda Chervin, *Spiritual Friendship: Darkness and Light* (Boston: Daughters of St. Paul, 1992), 19.

friends. We think our friend understands and loves us. Then something happens to breach the friendship.

Whenever our heart is pierced by the betrayal of a close friend, we can recall that Jesus was betrayed by one who enjoyed intimacy with His Sacred Heart. Providence could have arranged for anyone to play the protagonist, the betrayer. The Father ordained the betrayal to come from within the Lord's circle of closest friends.

That can happen to us also. It hurts very much. We know what we must do — forgive. We struggle. It is not easy. We want to justify our anger. We had hoped for a faithful friend. We can enter Gethsemane on that dark night of betrayal. We can see the Lord as He receives the kiss of His betrayer on His holy face. We cling to Christ, who has already paid the price of our pain. Then we forgive.

Profile in Mercy: St. John Paul II

It was May 13, 1981, and approximately twenty thousand people were gathered in Rome's St. Peter's Square for the papal audience. Pope John Paul II emerged with waves and smiles from the crowd. On this glorious Marian day in May, suddenly gunshots rang out. They came from an automatic pistol in the hands of Turkish Nationalist

Mehmet Ali Agca, who was attempting to assassinate the pope. The first bullet grazed the pope's elbow; the second pierced his side and entered his abdomen. The Holy Father fell back into the arms of his secretary, Fr. Stanislaw Dziwisz.

As he was bleeding profusely and in great danger of death, his automatic response was to speak to God; he prayed. He still had the presence of mind to know that it was 5 p.m. on May 13, the day the Virgin Mary appeared to three young children in Fátima. The Polish pope prayed for the help of Our Lady of Fátima. He had five abdominal wounds. The second bullet missed his main abdominal artery by a tenth of an inch. The pope spent five hours in surgery. Most people assumed he would die. Later he said, "I had a vision that I was to be saved."

When the pope came out of surgery, he asked to see the bullet that the surgeons had removed from his body. The Holy Father held it in his hand and instructed his staff to have the bullet grafted onto the crown of Mary in the shrine at Fátima, Portugal. In 2008, while on pilgrimage with the Carmelite Sisters, I visited Portugal's Fátima shrine and saw the bullet that is now mounted in the crown of Our Lady of Fátima. Providentially, there was a perfect-sized opening in her crown to receive the pope's bullet.

Two years later, during Christmas week of 1983, Pope John Paul II visited Rebibbia, the maximum-security prison in Italy, to meet with Agca. He told his would-be assassin that he forgave him. Before the meeting, the pope celebrated Mass with the prison inmates. Afterward, the Vicar of Christ sat for two hours in a plastic chair with the man who had tried to end his life.[1] Mercy triumphed gloriously. A saintly pope released the power of forgiving love that breaks down fear and hatred.

A merciful heart is able to do as Paul taught, "See that none of you repays evil for evil, but always seek to do good to one another and to all" (1 Thess. 5:15).

---

[1] Adapted from Allen R. Hunt's account in *Everybody Needs to Forgive Somebody: 11 Stories of People Who Discovered the Underrated Power of Grace*, 2nd ed. (Beacon Publishing, 2012).

Personal or Group Retreat Exercise

The Teaching of the Word of God
Read Luke 10:29–37: The Parable of the Good Samaritan.

But he, desiring to justify himself, said to Jesus, "And who is my neighbor?" Jesus replied, "A man was going down from Jerusalem to Jericho, and he fell among robbers, who stripped him and beat him, and departed, leaving him half dead. Now by chance a priest was going down that road; and when he saw him he passed by on the other side. So likewise a Levite, when he came to the place and saw him, passed by on the other side. But a Samaritan, as he journeyed, came to where he was; and when he saw him, he had compassion, and went to him and bound up his wounds, pouring on oil and wine; then he set him on his own beast and brought him to an inn, and took care of him. And the next day he took out two denarii and gave them to the innkeeper, saying, 'Take care of him; and whatever more you spend, I will repay you when I come back.' Which of these three, do you think, proved neighbor to the man who fell among the robbers?" He said, "The one who showed mercy on him." And Jesus said to him, "Go and do likewise."

QUESTIONS FOR GROUP OR PERSONAL REFLECTION

1. Have you ever acted like the Good Samaritan? Ponder the grace.

2. Were you ever on the receiving end of mercy, like the robber's victim? Who helped you?

3. Have you ever disregarded someone in need? If so, why? If not, what made you reach out?

4. Is there someone who treated you like the robber who hurt his victim? Invite Jesus into the wound and ask for the medicine of divine mercy.

5. Is there someone you consider to be your enemy? Ask Jesus what He wants you to do now.

Applying God's Mercy

God's Letter to You

Christ: My child, I have said: "Peace I leave with you, My peace I give to you. Not as the world gives do I give it to you" (Jn 14:27). All human beings desire peace; but not all will do what is necessary to obtain it. My peace is found among the humble and gentle of heart; you will find your peace by being patient. If you will listen to Me and follow My words, you will enjoy great peace.

At all times pay attention to what you are doing and what you are saying, and make it your constant intention to please Me alone, neither desiring nor seeking anything apart from Me. Do not make rash judgments on what others say or do, and do not concern yourself about things not committed to your care. If you follow this advice, you will be little or seldom disturbed. But never to feel any disturbance at all, nor to suffer any anguish of heart or bodily pain, is not the state of this present life, but of the life to come

Do not think, therefore, that you have found true peace if you feel no grief, nor that all is well if no one opposes you; nor that you have arrived at perfection if everything goes the way you want it.[26]

---

[26] Thomas à Kempis, *The Imitation of Christ* (New York: Catholic Book Publishing, 1977), 166.

Your Letter to God

5

RAYS OF DIVINE MERCY ON THE UNIVERSAL CHURCH: CLERGY, CONSECRATED, LAITY

Healing from Pride to Humility

✠

Wherever the Church is present, the mercy of the Father must be evident. In our parishes, communities, associations and movements, in a word, wherever there are Christians, everyone should find an oasis of mercy.

—Pope Francis, Bull of Indiction of the
Extraordinary Jubilee of Mercy, 12

We are the chosen, loved family of God, a community of believers, not a building, but a living body with Christ, our Head. St. Paul speaks of the unity of the Body of Christ: "If one member suffers, all suffer together; if one member is honored, all rejoice together. Now you are the body of Christ and individually members of it" (1 Cor. 12:26–27). The Church came forth from the pierced heart of Jesus, which gushed blood and water (cf. John 19:34); the wellspring of sacramental grace; the fount of mercy. If mercy is God's greatest attribute, could we not say then that mercy is the Church's greatest attribute also?

IN THIS CHAPTER

+ We will acknowledge the need for reparation as a response to God's mercy.

+ We will reflect on the need to heal from pride to humility.

+ We will consider true humility and its relationship to divine mercy.

The Church has been my merciful Mother throughout my lifetime. I have been taught, nurtured, strengthened, and loved by her. I have served her for most of my life, just as my good parents and their parents did. But I am a sinner in a community of sinners striving for holiness, although not always in the most Christ-like way. A community of sinners will hurt one another at times. This is where divine mercy enters to heal.

When we love Jesus Christ, He forms us to love His Church, since He loves her as the bridegroom loves a bride.

Reparation and Mercy Are Needed

Often, throughout the ages, members of the Church have responded to God's mercy with heroic virtue. Anyone who reads the Church Fathers and the accounts of the early Church martyrs finds a glorious history. Sometimes, however, the response of the Church's members to God's mercy has been anything but virtuous. There is a need for the sinful members of the Church to ask pardon and receive mercy from their victims also. In recent times the Church (through the last three popes) has offered apologies for the pain that we sinful members inflicted on too many people. Reparation is needed.[27] There is a need for the sinful members of the Church to ask pardon and receive mercy from their victims also.

God is infinitely patient and merciful with sinful disciples. Pride has been at work in us. Self-righteousness has manifested itself, and it is unattractive. Humility is needed. We have caused suffering to others and to one other. We are sinners striving to be Christ-like, but in truth we fall short of the ideal of the gospel. Yet we know many exemplary people of virtue, selfless servants of God, come from within our members. There is more that Christ asks of us, more that the world needs from us as God's ambassadors.

From Pride to Humility: "My House Shall Be a House of Prayer"

How can we be healed of the sin of pride to become a humble, merciful Church? Pride disguises itself in many ways. It's difficult to admit that some of our motives for good works can be rooted in pride. Sometimes what begins as a pure intention subtly changes into a prideful one. We must search our hearts for hidden pride.

The following points about the nature of pride are gleaned from St. Catherine of Siena's book *The Dialogue*.[28]

---

[27] "An offense against truth requires reparation" (CCC 2509).

[28] St. Catherine of Siena, *The Dialogue* (New York: Paulist Press, 1980), 80, 251.

+ Pride is born from and nurtured by sensual, inordinate self-love.

+ Pride obscures the knowledge of the truth.

+ Pride is the enemy of obedience.

+ Pride's pith is impatience.

+ Pride blinds the eye of the intellect.

+ Pride gives the appearance of tender self-love, but in truth it is cruel.

+ Pride causes the greatest poverty and misery.

+ Pride deprives of virtue and causes treacherous injustice.

+ Pride causes the elect to fall from heights to depths of mortal sin.

+ Pride is like a bandage over the eyes of the Spirit.

+ Pride perverts judgment.

Christ said, "It is written, 'My house shall be called a house of prayer'; but you make it a den of robbers" (Matt. 21:13). Is this the crux of the matter? Are we a Church that is "busy and anxious about so many things" (cf. Luke 10:41)? Many programs of catechesis and charitable works are necessary. Yet history reveals that *saints*, not programs, renew the Church. The universal call to holiness requires a contemplative foundation.

We are to be a spiritual edifice built on the foundation of prayer. This requires a life of *intentional prayer* centered on the Church's liturgical life. Liturgy is the Church's glorious heart from which flows divine mercy. But prayer is a battle that requires perseverance.

The *Catechism* explains:

Our battle has to confront what we experience as *failure in prayer*: discouragement during periods of dryness; sadness that, because we have "great possessions," we have not given all to the Lord; disappointment over not being heard according to our own will, wounded pride, stiffened by the indignity that is ours as sinners; our resistance to the idea that prayer is a free and unmerited gift; and so forth. The conclusion is always the same: what good does it do to pray? To overcome these obstacles, we must battle to gain humility, trust, and perseverance. (CCC 2728)

What Is True Humility?

The clearest picture of humility in history is Jesus Christ, who came to serve, not to be served (Matt. 20:28). He is the model of complete, authentic humility. Our attitude should be the same as that of Jesus, who "humbled himself and became obedient to death, even death on a cross" (Phil. 2:8).

We may fall short of this ideal until finally grace perfects us in humility. Undoubtedly, the crucifixion of our pride is painful, yet, for the sake of our conformity to Christ, we strive to become humble.

Besides, the virtue of humility imparts joy and freedom. In the *Catechism*, humility is defined as "the virtue by which a Christian acknowledges that God is the author of all good. Humility avoids inordinate ambition or pride, and provides the foundation for turning to God in prayer" (CCC 2559). Voluntary humility can be described as "poverty of spirit" (CCC 2546).

The practical Mother Teresa penned these ways to practice humility:[29]

+ to speak as little as possible of one's self

+ to mind one's own business

+ not to want to manage other people's affairs

+ to avoid curiosity

+ to accept contradictions and correction cheerfully

+ to pass over the mistakes of others

+ to accept insults and injuries

+ to accept being slighted, forgotten, and disliked

+ to be kind and gentle even under provocation

+ never to stand on one's dignity

+ to choose always the hardest

The Church battles enemies from within and without. Merciful love heals the ugliness of shame, sin, disgrace, and scandal. Divine mercy is hope, help, and happiness in our service to one another. Reflection on the words of St. John the Baptist, "He must increase, but I must decrease" (John 3:30), will guide the Church in the way of humility, on the path of merciful discipleship. The mission of every Christian is to manifest the merciful heart of Jesus Christ, in season and out of season, and without regard to the cost. Mercy is self-emptying love.

---

[29] Mother Teresa, *The Joy of Living: A Guide to Daily Living* (New York: Penguin Books, 2000), 406; posted at Good Reads, accessed June 16, 2015, http://www.goodreads.com/quotes/663304-these-are-the-few-ways-we-can-practice-humility-to.

Profile in Mercy: Cardinal Francis Xavier Nguyen Van Thuan, Prisoner of War

The following excerpts are from Cardinal Nguyen Van Thuan's testimony, *Experiencing God's Liberating Power*, prior to his death in 2002.[1]

On 15 August 1975, on the Feast of the Assumption of Our Lady, I was invited to the Palace of Independence, the President's Palace in Saigon, only to be arrested. The motive was that Pope Paul VI had transferred me from my diocese in Nha Trang where I had been bishop for eight years, between 1967 and 1975, to Saigon, to become Archbishop Coadjutor.

For the Communist Government this transfer, made one week before their arrival in Saigon, on 30 April 1975, was proof of a conspiracy between the Vatican and the "Imperialists". From the very first moment of my arrest, the words of Bishop John Walsh, who had been imprisoned for twelve years in Communist China, came to my mind. On

---

[1] Cardinal Francis Xavier Nguyen Van Thuan, "How Faith Survived in a Communist Prison," reprinted from *AD2000* 16, no. 4 (May 2003): 10; posted at Cardinal Francis Xavier Nguyen Van Thuan Foundation, accessed June 6, 2015, http://www.card-fxthuan.org/his-works/faith-survived-in-prison.php.

the day of his liberation Bishop Walsh said, "I have spent half my life waiting."

It is true. All prisoners, myself included, constantly wait to be let go. I decided then and there that my captivity would not be merely a time of resignation but a turning point in my life. I decided I would not wait. I would live the present moment and fill it with love. For if I wait, the things I wait for will never happen. The only thing that I can be sure of is that I am going to die.

No, I will not spend time waiting. I will live the present moment and fill it with love. Alone in my prison cell, I continued to be tormented by the fact that I was forty-eight years old, in the prime of my life, that I had worked for eight years as a bishop and gained so much pastoral experience and there I was isolated, inactive and far from my people.

One night, from the depths of my heart I could hear a voice advising me: "Why torment yourself? You must discern between God and the works of God—everything you have done and desire to continue to do, pastoral visits, training seminarians, sisters and members of religious orders, building schools, evangelizing non-Christians. All of that is excellent work, the work of God but it is not God! If God wants you to give it all up and put the work into his hands, do it and trust him. God will do the work infinitely better than you; he will entrust the work to others who are more able than you. You have only to choose God and not the works of God!"

This light totally changed my way of thinking. When the Communists put me in the hold of the boat, the

Hai-Phong, along with 1500 other prisoners and moved us to the North, I said to myself, "Here is my cathedral, here are the people God has given me to care for, here is my mission: to ensure the presence of God among these, my despairing, miserable brothers. It is God's will that I am here. I accept his will." And from that minute onwards, a new peace filled my heart and stayed with me for thirteen years.

I was taken to prison empty-handed. Later on, I was allowed to request the strict necessities like clothing, toothpaste, etc. I wrote home saying, "Send me some wine as medication for stomach pains." On the outside, the faithful understood what I meant. They sent me a little bottle of Mass wine, with a label reading "medication for stomach pains," as well as some hosts broken into small pieces. The police asked me: "Do you have pains in your stomach?" "Yes." "Here is some medicine for you!" I will never be able to express the joy that was mine: each day, with three drops of wine, a drop of water in the palm of my hand, I celebrated my Mass.

At night, the prisoners took turns and spent time in adoration. The Blessed Sacrament helped tremendously. Even Buddhists and other non-Christians were converted. The strength of the love of Jesus is irresistible. The darkness of the prison turned into light, the seed germinated silently in the storm.

When I began to discern between God and God's works, when I chose God and His will and left everything else in His hands, and when I learned to love others, especially my enemies as Jesus loved me, I felt great peace in my heart.

It was very hard for my guards to understand when I spoke about loving our enemies, reconciliation and forgiveness. "Do you really love us?" "Yes, I really love you." "Even when we cause you pain? When you suffer because you're in prison without trial?" "Look at all the years we've spent together. Of course, I love you!" "And when you get out, will you tell your people to find us and beat us and hurt our families?" "I'll continue to love you even if you wish to kill me." "But why?" "Because Jesus taught us to love always; if we don't, we are no longer worthy to be called Christians."

Personal or Group Spiritual Exercise

The Teaching of the Word of God
Read Acts 9:1–19: Saul's Conversion.

But Saul, still breathing threats and murder against the disciples of the Lord, went to the high priest and asked him for letters to the synagogues at Damascus, so that if he found any belonging to the Way, men or women, he might bring them bound to Jerusalem.

Now as he journeyed he approached Damascus, and suddenly a light from heaven flashed about him. And he fell to the ground and heard a voice saying to him, "Saul, Saul, why do you persecute me?" And he said, "Who are you, Lord?" And he said, "I am Jesus, whom you are persecuting; but rise and enter the city, and you will be told what you are to do." The men who were traveling with him stood speechless, hearing the voice but seeing no one.

Saul arose from the ground; and when his eyes were opened, he could see nothing; so they led him by the hand and brought him into Damascus. And for three days he was without sight, and neither ate nor drank.

Now there was a disciple at Damascus named Ananias. The Lord said to him in a vision, "Ananias." And he said, "Here I am, Lord." And the Lord said to him, "Rise and go to the street called Straight, and inquire in the house of Judas for a man of Tarsus named Saul; for behold, he is praying, and he has seen a man named Ananias come in and lay his hands on him so that he might regain his sight." But Ananias answered, "Lord, I have heard from many about this man, how much evil he has done to your saints at Jerusalem; and here he has authority from the chief priests to bind all who call upon your name." But the Lord said to him, "Go, for he is a chosen instrument of mine to carry my name before the Gentiles and kings and the sons of Israel; for I will show him how much he must suffer for the sake of my name."

So Ananias departed and entered the house. And laying his hands on him he said, "Brother Saul, the Lord Jesus who appeared to you on the road by which you came, has sent me that you may regain your sight and be filled with the Holy Spirit." And immediately something like scales fell from his eyes and he regained his sight. Then he rose and was baptized, and took food and was strengthened.

QUESTIONS FOR GROUP OR PERSONAL REFLECTION

1. Reflect on Saul's dramatic conversion. Has your encounter with Christ dramatically changed your life?

2. The conversion of Paul was an act of great divine mercy. Reflect on the greatest act of mercy that you received from God.

3. How has the Church blessed your life? What have you brought to the Church?

4. Is there someone you need to forgive in the Church? Ask Jesus to heal any wounds you may have and to lead you to true forgiveness.

5. Reflect on the journey from pride to humility. Ask Jesus to reveal how you can grow in humility and be rid of any pride.

Applying God's Mercy

God's Letter to You

Christ: Do not take it seriously, my child, if people think evil of you and say things about you that you do not want to hear. You ought to have a worse opinion of yourself and to think that no one is weaker than you.

If you are well recollected within, you will take no notice of fleeting words from without. It is a sign of wisdom, when evil words are spoken, to keep silence and to turn your heart to Me, refusing to be disturbed by man's judgment.

Do not let your peace of mind depend on what people say about you. You are still what you are, no matter whether they put a good or bad interpretation on your actions. Where will you find true peace and true glory if not in Me?

Certainly this is so. The person who never aspires to please others nor fears to displease them will enjoy much peace; for all disquiet of heart and distraction of the senses come from disorderly affections and groundless fear.[30]

Your Letter to God

---

[30] Thomas à Kempis, *The Imitation of Christ*, 174.

6

RAYS OF DIVINE MERCY ON OUR VARIOUS VOCATIONS

Healing from No to Yes

Mary is also the one who obtained mercy, in a particular and exceptional way, as no other person has. At the same time, still in an exceptional way, she made possible with the sacrifice of her heart her own sharing in revealing God's mercy.

—John Paul II, *Dives in Misericordia*

Struggling, humanity waited with hope for centuries. Then the merciful Triune God made an astonishing and utterly unpredictable move. In the fullness of time, the Savior was sent from heaven to earth to heal humanity of sin, evil, and death. Jesus Christ, the only-begotten Son of the Father, said yes to the plan first. He would become the Divine Mercy to heal the original wound inflicted by Adam and Eve.

But the yes of another person would be required. Mary's yes to God would forever change the course of human history. Absent the "original wound," she was chosen to be the New Eve. Humanity needed a new Eve because the original woman of the Garden of Eden said no to God instead of yes. Saying no to

IN THIS CHAPTER

+ We will reflect upon Mary's yes so that we can make an intentional fiat to God and better discern His will for our vocations.

+ We will renounce the times we refused God's invitations, gifts, and call and pray for healing.

+ We will consider the constancy of our yes to God and the self-emptying love required for our vocation.

God is never a good idea. The consequences are real and serious. Mary's yes healed Eve's no to God. Mary's yes to God is rooted in her humble, obedient heart attuned to God's word. Eve's no to God was rooted in prideful, disobedient independence from God. With her yes, Mary became the Mother of Divine Mercy, the handmaid of the Divine Physician. The Church, born of a dual yes — God's and Mary's — is the hospital of mercy. Many are the wounds caused by our no to God that result in infidelity to our vocation, independence from God, and disobedience to His will.

Yes to God: Surrender, Sacrifice, and Self-Emptying

At the Twenty-Eighth World Youth Day in Rio de Janeiro, on Sunday, July 28, 2013, Pope Francis said, "Go and make disciples of all nations.... Jesus is calling you to be a disciple with a mission!" The faithful have a mission to proclaim the Good News of Jesus Christ. The proclamation of the kingdom, like sanctity, is not the privilege of a few but the call and duty of every disciple. How we go about proclaiming Christ to others depends on our vocation in life.

Whether we are called to priesthood or to the religious life, to consecrated or married life, our yes is key to the fulfillment of God's design for our life. Foundational to all vocations is falling in love with Jesus and staying in love with Him. If you have not had the experience of falling in love with Jesus, ask God for the grace. Your desire is born of His desire. Let your mutual yes create the fire of divine love within you. The greater the fire within, the more you radiate Christ.

When we ponder the vocation of Mary, we can begin to understand that she led the way for us to be open to the surprising adventure of God's call in our life. Like Mary we are chosen for something far greater than what has entered our mind. God's love is dynamic. He seeks to work small and big miracles of grace through us. Yet the God of love will not burst through our free will and force us to respond to Him.

The singular mission of Mary was God's idea, not hers. This is an important reminder that He has a plan, a mission within a vocation for each person. The vocation of each believer includes a call that we magnify Jesus Christ in the world. Various vocations share a common calling: transformation in Christ. Clergy and laity are called to be Christ-bearers. Mary's yes to the Trinity required a decision to surrender, self-empty, and sacrifice to birth Jesus, the Incarnate Word, into the world. She surrendered her previous plan in favor of His. She emptied herself so that God could fill her. She became a sacrifice of praise to God. Mary's Magnificat is much more than her hymn of praise to the Trinity.

It is her *identity*. Mary is the embodiment of the Magnificat. How does this relate to our vocation? Because of Christ's yes and Mary's yes, our identity as a child of God is realized. Our yes to the Lord is key to our identity also.

The Healing Journey from No to Yes

Consider Adam and Eve's no to God. The result is that the false self emerged, the self that wants to hide from God and run away in shame. Our yes to God binds us to Him so that we are unbound from what is not God. Saying no to God wounds the Church and the world. Many people say no to God by refusing the gift of children. Abortion is one of the wounds of that no. Numerous couples say no to sacramental marriage and cohabitate instead. Fornication is the wound of that no. Countless people say no to fidelity in marriage, and the wound of that no is adultery. Some priests say no to their priesthood and the wound of that no is scandal. Some young people refuse God's call to the priesthood and consecrated life, and the wound of that no is empty rectories and convents. Most people have experienced the negative impact of someone's no to God. As with Adam and Eve's no, there are negative consequences.

A Prayer for the Grace to Say Yes to God
Lord Jesus, You have helped me to understand that I am not fully surrendered to Your will in my life. My self-will is strong, and I am capable of little steps only. By grace I have come to understand that You desire the totality of my yes.

I repent of the times when, knowingly or unknowingly, I interfered with Your plan for my life either by neglect in prayer, procrastination in doing what You asked, fear of making a wrong decision, of letting go of options that make me feel that I have control of my life.

You have led me on a journey across hills and valleys that I could not foresee. I would not have chosen such a difficult path. You knew that, of course. That the cross is so much a part of the journey is a signal grace of the magnitude of Your plan for good.

With all my heart I ask for the healing that I need; the healing of wounds that are the result of folly, the healing of my heart that I protect, the healing of my thoughts that were not Your thoughts. With the full strength of my free will, I now offer my unreserved yes to You. Thank You for your patience, providence, and peace. Only Your will be done in my life. I am yours, and with You I am safe.

Every vocation exists to bring forth Jesus Christ in the world. What if Mary had not responded at the appointed time of the Annunciation? How many times have we failed to respond to the invitation of God? Unique to the Virgin Mary is an unencumbered yes to God that is permanent and courageous. Was Mary free to say no to God? Minus original sin, she is absolutely free. She made a true decision of her will. Even when her yes cost the agony of accompanying her Son, Jesus, bone of her bone, flesh of her flesh, to His cruel death by crucifixion, every atom of her being remained in complete accord with the yes of her Son.

Mary is the icon of fidelity to God. Every child of God, every person on earth, from start to finish throughout human history, is the beneficiary of Mary's yes. The Lord's yes and His creature Mary's yes interlocked to heal the family of man. Our yes to God is fundamental to our salvation. Mary took a leap of faith, and this is foundational to every yes, every vocation.

The Constancy of Your Yes to God and the Truth about Your Vocation

The Church offers several aids in the discernment of one's vocation. Even after the vocation decision is made and the vocation is lived out for years, it is necessary to discern important life-impacting decisions. The renowned Spiritual Exercises of St. Ignatius of Loyola are one of the foremost methods of discernment offered by the Church. The Ignatian method of discernment has saved me from making incredibly serious mistakes in judgment regarding marriage and family. In the second week of the Spiritual Exercises, St. Ignatius teaches that there are certain things that fall under an unchangeable choice, such as priesthood and marriage. Once one has made a choice (by proceeding to priestly ordination or exchanging marriage vows), no further choice is possible. The founder of the Jesuits also said: "If the choice has not been made as it should have been, and with due order, that is, if it was not made without inordinate attachments, one should be sorry for this, and take care to live well in the life he has chosen."[31]

We know there are spiritual exercises for discernment that are effective. The challenge is not with the process of discernment as much as it is with our perception of a vocation. In the present narcissistic culture, filled with false promises of complete happiness and fulfillment based on everything *but* the gospel of Jesus, we fail to arrive at a complete yes to God because of our self-concerns, preferences, and failure to commit to anything that is lifelong, sacrificial, or less thrilling than the exciting transitory

---

[31] *The Spiritual Exercises of St. Ignatius*, trans. Louis J. Puhl (Chicago: Loyola Press, 1951), nos. 171–172.

allurements of the world and the devil. Contrast these with the persistent call of Jesus to serve Him and others in humility and self-emptying love.

Now vocational discernment becomes anxiety ridden and full of unnecessary procrastination to make a commitment at all. We live in a consumer culture obsessed with countless options for the pursuit of happiness, most of which do not mention words such as "deny yourself, take up your cross daily, and follow me" (cf. Luke 9:23). Whether we realize it or not, our expectations are simply unrealistic, and they can set us up for nothing but failure and disappointment.

All Vocations Are Self-Emptying

Whether the vocation is to the priesthood, religious life, marriage, or single life, the vocation itself is not meant to fulfill that God-shaped hole in our heart. Sometimes we seek heaven on earth and become angry that we do not find it. Any vocation has as its purpose the way of dying to self, imitating Christ in His self-emptying love, and loving God and others in the humble posture of a servant of God. As Jesus and Mary were faithful to the end of their missions for the sake of love, we are called to commit, work, serve, and love selflessly in our vocations.

God's will is usually the harder choice, the more difficult path; the one that requires more of Him and less of me. No vocation is the fulfillment of all human desire. Only God fulfills. That is why it is necessary to fall in love and stay in love with Christ. Our vocations are not meant to solve the mystery of human life, love, and longing. Vocations are where we work out our salvation while keeping our eyes fixed on Christ and heaven. The answer to our human longing will be forthcoming in the Father's house, not on earth. On earth we walk by faith, hope, and love; we toil and press on amid temptations and trials. Merciful love is strong, capable of great things, capable of withstanding the cross.

Profile in Mercy: Mary at the Foot of the Cross

In January 2013, locked inside the Church of the Holy Sepulchre in Jerusalem for prayer, I set my heart on Christ's Passion and death. Placing my hand on Calvary's surface, I contrasted the cold, hard rock with the warmth of the Sacred Heart aflame with love's passion. In the pangs of death by crucifixion, His heart was entirely kindled with the fire that He longed to start on earth. He was ready to offer His heart to be pierced, desirous of opening His sacred side to be the mercy fountain of water and blood that would gush over humanity to redeem it. To paraphrase St. Augustine, "What sacrifice can I offer to God worthy of His mercy?"

In contemplation I could almost hear the cacophony of the murderous crowd at Calvary and the contrasting peaceful, steady rhythm of the heart of Jesus. How very perfect is His sacrifice! It became incredibly personal: I crucified Him, and it was for me that He suffered and died. I pondered whether I would have remained near the Cross with Mary and John the beloved, with Magdalene and the other holy women. Would I have run away in fear with the first apostles? The mystery remains, but of this I became certain. If I had remained at the foot of the Cross at Calvary, it would have been because of Mary's maternal solicitude.

I would have looked into Mary's eyes for a sign, a cue of sorts. I can't imagine that I would run away in fear if I had looked into the eyes of the Mother of the Crucified One, ever faithful and courageous. One faith-filled look from Mary would have helped to plant my feet steadfastly at the foot of the Cross. Gazing into Mary's eyes mirroring the Lord, I would have known that the abyss between heaven and earth was about to be bridged by the Cross upon which hung Jesus.

Looking at Mary so full of love, and knowing that she was looking back at me, coaching me in virtue, protecting me from cowardice, I would have believed and hoped against all appearances of failure. I would have taken my mind off myself and focused on what was really happening here: the redemption of the world! Mary's loving gaze would have reminded me of her Son's words: "So you have sorrow now, but I will see you again and your hearts will rejoice, and no one will take your joy from you" (John 16:22). The Mother of Mercy would urge me to join in her hymn of praise, the Magnificat.

Although her holy face would be wet with tears and her heart seven times pierced with sorrow, Mary is the perfect icon of fidelity, courage, and love in the midst of the un-fathomable sacrifice of Jesus. Here hangs Mary's Son, the God-Man disfigured by the brutality of sin, urging the Father to forgive His executioners. Here stands Mary, in unspeakable pain, full of grace, without fear or shame, full of hope. The Mother of Mercy forgives her Son's murderers too. Her feet firmly planted on the rock of Calvary, she knows the time of salvation has come. Was she relieved when Jesus said to Abba, "It is finished" (John 19:30)? Perhaps. But in her wise maternal heart she must have known that Christ's mission of mercy was truly beginning.

Personal or Group Spiritual Exercise

The Teaching of the Word of God
Read Luke 1:26–38: The Annunciation.

In the sixth month the angel Gabriel was sent from God to a city of Galilee named Nazareth, to a virgin betrothed to a man whose name was Joseph, of the house of David; and the virgin's name was Mary. And he came to her and said, "Hail, full of grace, the Lord is with you!" But she was greatly troubled at the saying, and considered in her mind what sort of greeting this might be. And the angel said to her, "Do not be afraid, Mary, for you have found favor with God. And behold, you will conceive in your womb and bear a son, and you shall call his name Jesus. He will be great, and will be called the Son of the Most

High; and the Lord God will give to him the throne of his father David, and he will reign over the house of Jacob for ever; and of his kingdom there will be no end."

And Mary said to the angel, "How can this be, since I have no husband?" And the angel said to her, "The Holy Spirit will come upon you, and the power of the Most High will overshadow you; therefore the child to be born will be called holy, the Son of God. And behold, your kinswoman Elizabeth in her old age has also conceived a son; and this is the sixth month with her who was called barren. For with God nothing will be impossible." And Mary said, "Behold, I am the handmaid of the Lord; let it be to me according to your word." And the angel departed from her.

QUESTIONS FOR GROUP OR PERSONAL REFLECTION

1. Like Mary, are you responding to God's call to something greater than yourself? If so, how?

2. Contrast the outcome of your yes versus no to God's will in your life.

3. Reflect on a time you said no to God. Consider the root cause; for example, fear. Pray for healing.

4. Reflect on Mary at the foot of the Cross. How have you been helped by the example of her steadfast yes to God?

5. How are you growing in self-emptying love by means of your vocation?

Applying God's Mercy

God's Letter to You

My child, make the resolution never to rely on people. Entrust yourself completely to My will, saying, "Not as I want, but according to Your will, O God, let it be done unto me." These words, spoken from the depths of one's heart, can raise a soul to the summit of sanctity in a short time. In such a soul I delight. Such a soul gives Me glory. Such a soul fills heaven with the fragrance of her virtue. But understand that the strength by which you bear sufferings comes from frequent Communions. So approach this fountain of mercy often, to draw with the vessel of trust whatever you need.

My child, know that the greatest obstacles to holiness are discouragement and an exaggerated anxiety. These will deprive you of the ability to practice virtue. All temptations united together ought not disturb your interior peace, not even momentarily. Sensitiveness and discouragement are the fruits of self-love. You should not become discouraged, but strive to make My love reign in place of your self-love. Have confidence, My child. Do not lose heart in coming for pardon, for I am always ready to forgive you. As often as you beg for it, you glorify My mercy.[32]

---

[32] St. Faustina, *Diary*, nos. 1487, 1488.

Your Letter to God

7

RAYS OF DIVINE MERCY ON DOUBTERS AND BELIEVERS

Healing from Powerlessness to Prayer

✠

*The situation of the world today not only displays transformations
that give grounds for hope in a better future for man on earth,
but also reveals the multitude of threats far surpassing those
known up till now. . . . And this is why, in the situation of the
Church and the world today, many individuals and groups
guided by a lively sense of faith are turning, I would
say almost spontaneously, to the mercy of God.*

—Pope John Paul II, *Dives in Misericordia*

We place our hope in the God of mercy even as the modern culture offers decreasing support for Catholicism. There are not a few people who have gone from belief to doubt. But we are the people God has chosen for the present threats.

In Acts we read, "And the Lord said to Paul one night in a vision, 'Do not be afraid, but speak and do not be silent; for I am with you, and no man shall attack you to harm you; for I have many people in this city'" (Acts 18:9–10). Christ has many friends still.

IN THIS CHAPTER

+ We will distinguish between powerlessness and Pauline weakness.

+ We will seek to be healed from powerlessness to prayer power.

+ We will learn to release the healing power of prayer.

The threats that we experience from within and without cause many people to experience the powerlessness that leads to unbelief. Too many believers seem to be wavering precisely when we need to exercise vibrant faith, hope, and love. Often I ask, "Do I place my faith in the secular news or in the good news of Jesus Christ?" The Church is "city set on a hill [that] cannot be hidden. Nor do men light a lamp and put it under a bushel, but on a stand, and it gives light to all in the house. Let your light so shine before men" (Matt. 5:14–16). What if we are the people whom St. Louis de Montfort wrote about in his Marian opus, "They shall thunder against sin; they shall storm against the world; they shall strike the devil and his crew; and they shall pierce through and through, for life or for death, with their two-edged sword of the Word of God"?[33]

As a Catholic missionary who travels extensively to many cities and countries, I have discovered that strong adherence to the Divine Mercy devotion contributes to faithful Catholic cells that are beacons of light in the darkness. In Aruba I met women

---

[33] St. Louis de Montfort, *True Devotion to Mary* (Rockford, IL: TAN Books, 1985), no. 57.

whose children have succumbed to the unrelenting drug lords and are now addicts. These women refuse to give up, and they strengthen one another at Mass and Adoration, and by together praying the Rosary and the Chaplet of Divine Mercy. Some of their children are rescued. They trust exceedingly in God's mercy while others see no reason for hope.

In Trinidad I met a joyful eighty-year-old priest who, with a radiant smile, shared that he pastors seven parishes. He asked me to pray with him because his back aches from fatigue. He fasts for his parishioners and sleeps little because they can, and do, call him at any time. He becomes part of their family as a spiritual father. The Trinidadians refer to him as "the Curé of Trinidad." There are signs of hope everywhere amid the many threats of the modern world.

Distinguishing between Powerlessness and Pauline Weakness

Instinctively, we believers turn to the mercy of God when we feel threatened. Are we not children reaching for our heavenly Father? Catholics face goliath issues such as global and homeland terrorism, increasing civil and domestic violence, sexual promiscuity that tears at the fabric of Christian morality, a culture of death with abortion, euthanasia, and increased violence and suicide, civil laws that redefine marriage, and educational systems with anti-Catholic agendas. The Church, at least in the United States, is embroiled in lawsuits to defend Catholic hospitals, charities, and dioceses.

We can begin to live with a sense of powerlessness in an anti-Christian modern world in which we feel threatened. We may feel like a small cog in a large wheel and become paralyzed spiritually or emotionally.

Powerlessness can set in when we become discouraged by events that mystify us or test our faith. For example, we are deeply shaken (and rightfully so) when our children reject the Faith of our family or when we discover that our spouse is addicted to pornography and acting out to the detriment of the marriage. Too often, children are expected to be superstars, and those who cannot cope may escape into drugs, sex, or alcohol. We are hurt and scandalized by the actions of a few clergy in the abuse of minors. We feel the weight of cosmic sin that wounds our heart. The Holy Spirit makes us sensitive to such spiritual realities. We are weak with the weakness that St. Paul preaches. But the powerlessness of lethargy and discouragement is a temptation.

A distinction should be made between the powerlessness that I am referring to and the weakness that St. Paul refers to in his second letter to the Corinthians. St. Paul writes, "For the sake of Christ, then, I am content with weaknesses, insults, hardships, persecutions, and calamities; for when I am weak, then I am strong" (2 Cor. 12:10). In the same letter he writes, "If I must boast, I will boast of the things that show my weakness" (2 Cor. 11:30). This Pauline weakness is necessary so that Christ's strength can be manifested in and through us. We are weak but not paralyzed to live the gospel despite the threats of the world and evil.

Powerlessness That Paralyzes

The powerlessness that can paralyze Christians is a sense of loss, loss of zeal for the Faith, loss of hope, loss of Catholic purpose, loss of real love for God. Then lethargy and discouragement rule the day rather than trust, hope, and passion for God. A sense of powerlessness is not uncommon among members of the Church. The result is that some convert from belief to doubt, from hope to despair, from mercy to anger, from joy to sadness.

Such powerlessness can cause us to disengage from the hard conversation of defending the Faith in the public square or among family and friends. By defending the Faith I am not implying that we necessarily do so as apologists and catechists, because few Catholics consider themselves such. I am referring to bearing witness by our intentional discipleship, life, and prayer and engaging in the telling of our Catholic stories for the edification of others—as did the women of Aruba whom I mentioned earlier.

Another effect of negative powerlessness is the cessation of prayer and even sacramental life. Often there is not a deliberate decision to cease prayer or the sacraments. Rather, there is a slow progression from not praying for one or two days, and then for a month, and a year, and so forth. The same is true for the sacraments. Sunday Mass is omitted occasionally, then more often. A disconnection occurs and we become Catholic in name only. If prayer and sacraments cease, how do we experience the love of God? We can pray against the temptation to powerlessness, ask to be healed, and release the power of prayer instead.

Healing from Powerlessness to Prayer

It may be helpful to consider the powerlessness to which Judas succumbed when, *unlike Peter*, he could not accept the mercy of

God. When he finally realized the immense wrong he had done in betraying the Lord, was there a moment for repentance or conversion of heart? Did he not take things into his own hands in the despairing moment when he put his neck into the noose? What if he had turned to the Mother of Christ for help? We must be vigilant because we have an enemy who seeks to seduce us into the despair of Judas. The temptation begins with small betrayals, infidelities to smaller duties, and then bigger ones.

Prayer for Healing

Lord Jesus Christ, I beseech You to release me from the powerlessness that has gripped me to the detriment of my faith, hope, and love. I repent of having succumbed to such depth of powerlessness that I could no longer see the truth of Your power, victory, and mercy in a world of threats. My Redeemer, please forgive my lack of trust in You. Help me never again to look at the threats to my life and world without seeing that You are present in everything; that Divine Mercy is at work in the midst of darkness and light; that everywhere You have friends of the gospel who are engaged in extending Your Kingdom. I acknowledge that You want me to turn to You immediately in the face of all temptations.

I believe that You come to meet me now, where I am, in the dwelling place of my heart. I humble myself before Your majesty. Thank You for lifting me up from the dust and encouraging me to tell You everything that is on my mind. I speak to You of the needs of the Church, of the souls of poor sinners like me, of families besieged with problems, and of clergy in need of special grace. Lord, You graciously heal my wounds. Moreover, Your Spirit fills me with renewed faith, hope, and love and the courage to begin again in Your holy

Name. Jesus, please transform my sense of powerlessness, discouragement, and doubt into the healing power of prayer.

The Power of Prayer

In this brief reflection, a full teaching on prayer is not possible, so I'll offer a few relevant points. However, accessible to everyone is the brilliant catechesis on Christian Prayer in the *Catechism*.[34]

The Holy Spirit gives power to prayer. I never assume that I know how to pray and am always aware of the Spirit's abiding desire to pray within me. I invoke the Holy Spirit countless times a day: *Come, Holy Spirit.* I deliberately ask the Holy Spirit to release the power of His prayer in and through me. It is a joy to be led by the Holy Spirit because He makes prayer dynamic. If you cannot relate to this experience yet, please ask the Holy Spirit to release in you the power of His prayer.

When we are convinced of the power of prayer, we pray with expectant faith. We must pray, then, as Mary did at Cana when she said to the waiters, "Do whatever He tells you"—she fully expected her prayer to be answered!

We must face in ourselves and around us "erroneous notions of prayer". Some people view prayer as a simply psychological activity, others as an effort of concentration to reach a mental void. Still others reduce prayer to ritual words and postures. Many Christians unconsciously regard prayer as an occupation that is incompatible with

---

[34] See part 4 of the *Catechism*, on Christian Prayer: http://www.vatican.va/archive/ENG0015/_INDEX.HTM.

all the other things they have to do: they "don't have the time." Those who seek God by prayer are quickly discouraged because they do not know that prayer comes also from the Holy Spirit and not from themselves alone. (CCC 2726)

We can cultivate the holy habit of abiding in communion with the Divine Mercy by means of prayer. "The life of prayer is the habit of being in the presence of the thrice-holy God and in communion with him" (CCC 2565). The rays of divine mercy draw us up into the *life* of the Trinity. Engulfed in the dynamism of Trinitarian life, we become healed and sanctified.

The foundation of all prayer is humility. We approach God out of the depths of a humble, contrite heart, not from the height of pride or will. "Man is a beggar before God" (CCC 2559). The thirst for God initiates prayer. Our response satisfies the mutual thirst of Creator and creature. Prayer is relationship. Primary is the Church's liturgical prayer, the Mass, and the Liturgy of the Hours. Personal prayer follows with Adoration, *lectio divina*, devotional prayer such as the Rosary, the Chaplet of Divine Mercy, praise, gratitude, intercession, petition, meditation, and then the gift of contemplation—silent infused prayer.

When we awaken to the Holy Spirit's power praying within us, we begin to understand the correlation between love and prayer. Have you noticed how much easier it is to pray for those we love most? Parents who pray for their children do so with ardent love. I pray often and intensely but not always with the fullness of love. I must invoke the Holy Spirit because He releases divine love into prayer. Intentional discipleship demands authentic prayer: (1) sit at the feet of the Master; (2) absorb His merciful love; (3) become like Him in loving and serving others.

Prayer dispels powerlessness and empowers us to become vessels of divine mercy.

Profile in Mercy: St. Maria Goretti

Maria was born in Nettuno, Italy, twenty miles outside Rome, on October 16, 1890. Her father was a farmer who moved his family to Ferrier di Conca, near Anzio. He died of malaria when Maria was nine years old, and her mother was left to struggle to feed her children. In 1902, Alessandro, an eighteen-year-old neighbor who helped on the farm, grabbed hold of eleven-year-old Maria and tried to rape her. Maria said that she would rather die than submit. Or perhaps her concern about *his* purity motivated her resistance. Alessandro began stabbing her with a knife and inflicted fourteen stab wounds. In the hospital, she forgave Alessandro before she died. However, her death did not end her act of forgiveness.

Her attacker was captured and sentenced to thirty years. He remained unrepentant until he had a dream that he was in a garden, and Maria appeared and gave him fourteen roses, one for each stab wound. When he awoke, Alessandro was a changed man. He reformed his life and repented of his crime against Maria. He was released after twenty-seven years in prison and immediately went to

Maria's mother to beg forgiveness, and she forgave him. She said, "If my daughter can forgive him, who am I to withhold forgiveness?" After his jail time Alessandro was admitted to a monastery, where he did menial tasks. Maria was merciful to Alessandro, who in turn accepted mercy. And once he accepted her forgiveness, he retracted his story that she was the aggressor; this permitted her cause of canonization to move forward.

In 1950, when Pope Pius XII declared Maria Goretti a saint, Alessandro was in the crowd in St. Peter's Square to celebrate her canonization, next to Maria's mother. What a marvelous living portrait of divine mercy! Can you imagine yourself doing the same? Maria was canonized for her purity as a model for youth and is called a martyr because she fought to the death against Alessandro's attempts at sexual assault. The vital point of this story is the forgiveness of Maria, who is a vessel of divine mercy. Her feast day is July 6, and she is considered the patroness of youth and of victims of rape. Alessandro, who had killed Maria, repented and changed his life thanks to the mercy shown by her.

This story illustrates the power of *giving* and of *accepting* forgiveness. Both are necessary for healing. In today's climate of legal contentiousness and desire only for justice, would Maria and Alessandro's situation have a chance of playing out as it did gloriously in their time? Are we crowding out mercy?

Personal or Group Spiritual Exercise

The Teaching of the Word of God
Read Matthew 8:5–10: Jesus heals the Centurion's servant.

As he entered Capernaum, a centurion came forward to him, begging him and saying, "Lord, my servant is lying paralyzed at home, in terrible distress." And he said to him, "I will come and heal him." But the centurion answered him, "Lord, I am not worthy to have you come under my roof; but only say the word, and my servant will be healed. For I am a man under authority, with soldiers under me; and I say to one, 'Go,' and he goes, and to another, 'Come,' and he comes, and to my slave, 'Do this,' and he does it." When Jesus heard him, he marveled, and said to those who followed him, "Truly, I say to you, not even in Israel have I found such faith. I tell you, many will come from east and west and sit at table with Abraham, Isaac, and Jacob in the kingdom of heaven, while the sons of the kingdom will be thrown into the outer darkness; there men will weep and gnash their teeth." And to the centurion Jesus said, "Go; let it be done for you as you have believed." And the servant was healed at that very moment.

QUESTIONS FOR GROUP OR PERSONAL REFLECTION

1. What do these words, based on those of the centurion: "Lord, only say the word and my soul shall be healed?" mean to you personally?

2. Jesus is amazed at the centurion's faith level. What would Jesus think of your faith level? Ask the Lord for more faith.

3. Jesus healed the centurion's servant. Thankfully recall the times when Jesus healed you. Ask for the healing you may still need.

4. If you experience powerlessness, pray to transform your powerlessness into the power of faith-filled prayer.

5. How is doubt negatively affecting your relationship with Christ? Decide to trust in God.

Applying God's Mercy

God's Letter to You

I want to instruct you on how you are to rescue souls through sacrifice and prayer. You will save more souls through prayer and suffering than will a missionary through his teachings and sermons alone. I want to see you as a sacrifice of living love, which only then carries weight before Me. . . . And great will be your power for whomever you intercede. Outwardly, your sacrifice must look like this: silent, hidden, permeated with love, imbued with prayer. . . . You shall accept all sufferings with love. Do not be afflicted if your heart often experiences repugnance and dislike for sacrifice. All its power rests in the will, and so these contrary feelings, far from lowering the value of your sacrifice in my eyes, will enhance it. Although you will not feel My presence on some occasions, I will always be with you. Do not fear; My grace will be with you.[35]

Your Letter to God

---

[35] St. Faustina, *Diary*, nos. 1767, 1768.

8

RAYS OF MERCY ON PEOPLE WITH DIABOLICAL SUFFERING

Healing from Spiritual Warfare to Christ's Victory

✠

What are the Church's greatest needs at the present time?
Don't be surprised at our answer and don't write it off as simplistic
or even superstitious: one of the Church's greatest needs is
to be defended against the evil we call the Devil.

Pope Paul VI, General Audience, November 15, 1972

In the Gospels, Jesus, Chief Exorcist, generously exercises mercy in His deliverance ministry. We have recourse to Christ in every diabolical trial as we wrestle with ordinary temptation or occasional cases of extraordinary spiritual warfare. Christ underwent the devil's temptations in the desert to teach us how to resist demonic seductions.

Spiritual warfare, a trial and test of faith, is part of authentic discipleship. Daily temptations challenge us to resist the demonic. We are not dealing with magic, phantasm, or abstract negative "energy" when we speak about demons, the devil, Satan, or Lucifer.

IN THIS CHAPTER

+ We will consider God's mercy for people with diabolical suffering and how to resist demonic attacks.

+ We will distinguish between ordinary and extraordinary spiritual warfare.

+ We will consider divine mercy in twelve spiritual
  weapons of protection and pray for healing.

"Evil is not an abstraction, but refers to a person, Satan, the evil
one, the angel who opposes God. The devil is the one who 'throws
himself across' God's plan and his work of salvation" (CCC 2851).

In the mystery of God's infinite wisdom, Satan is allowed to
operate in the world within the boundaries set by the sovereign
Holy Trinity. Every Christian is put to the test and is called to be
a soldier for Christ, as Paul wrote to Timothy, "Take your share
of suffering as a good soldier of Christ Jesus" (2 Tim. 2:3). God
can use spiritual warfare for the perfection of our faith. Love is
fire tested. The devil tempts so that he may ruin; God tests so
that He may crown, to paraphrase St. Ambrose of Milan.

In *Dives in Misericordia*, Pope John Paul II, referring to the
parable of the prodigal son (Luke 15:11–32), writes, "Mercy — as
Christ has presented it in the parable of the prodigal son — has
the interior form of the love that in the New Testament is called
agape. This love is able to reach down to every prodigal son, to
every human misery, and above all to every form of moral misery,
to sin. When this happens, the person who is the object of mercy
does not feel humiliated, but rather found again and 'restored to
value.' The father first and foremost expresses to him his joy that

he has been 'found again' and that he has 'returned to life'" (no. 6). This articulates divine mercy operative in the Church's healing, deliverance and exorcism ministry. Merciful love restores.

God's Mercy for Resisting Demons

Why does the God of mercy ordain a spiritual battle for His people on earth? Christ's words to St. Faustina lend understanding: "But child, you are not yet in your homeland; so go, fortified by My grace, and fight for My kingdom in human souls; fight as a king's child would; and remember the days of your exile will pass quickly, and with them the possibility of earning merit for heaven. I expect from you, My child, a great number of souls who will glorify My mercy for all eternity."[36] Christ taught St. Faustina a principle that applies to all believers. A greater number of souls will eternally glorify the Divine Mercy because they received mercy in the way that David did in the defeat of Goliath (cf. 1 Sam. 17).

Scott Hahn explains, "Demon is the name applied to all varieties of evil spirits, including the devil or Satan. Demons like angels, are pure spirits, which means they do not have bodies and are invisible; nevertheless, they sometimes manipulate or possess a human or animal body (cf. Gen 3:13–15; Isa 34:14)."[37]

Demons are real, numerous, malicious, and cunning. Cases of possession are rare but are increasing due to growing membership in various forms of Satanism. I offer my observation as one who has witnessed many rites of exorcism as part of a team serving a

---

[36] St. Faustina, *Diary*, no. 1489.

[37] Scott Hahn, *Catholic Bible Dictionary* (New York: Doubleday, 2009), 210.

variety of exorcists. I was called into the Church's healing and deliverance ministry fifteen years ago at the invitation of priests and my bishop. After ten years of training at conferences for priests and laity who are serving in deliverance ministry, I was enlisted as a facilitator and spiritual director for the Pope Leo XIII Institute for Priests. Hollywood movies about exorcism cannot convey the real mystical presence and power of Jesus, Chief Exorcist at work in His Church.

Hahn writes, "Chief among the demons was Satan. He is the judicial adversary or accuser in Job (Job 1:6ff., 2:1ff.; cf. Zech. 3:1), and the chief evil spirit, tempter who took the form of the serpent in Gen 3 (Wis 2:24). In the New Testament, demons—also called unclean spirits, evil spirits, and similar names—are an assumed reality. They are servants of evil, the angels of Satan, determined to tempt and destroy humanity and to spread evil and suffering in the world."[38]

The Enemy's ordinary activity is to ruin souls through a variety of temptations. Demons strategize for the soul's damnation, but they cannot violate our free will; they seduce but cannot force. The decision and responsibility are ours. By observation they can determine our weakest area of resistance. Sinful habits such as pornography, inordinate gambling or alcohol, gluttony, adultery, and so forth make us more vulnerable. Evil spirits enter through the misuse or weakness of the five senses: sight, hearing, taste, touch, and smell. They also exit through these portals of the soul at the time of deliverance.

When we overcome temptation, we are strengthened in virtue, advance God's kingdom, and defeat evil. Our faith life is a spiritual battle (CCC 2726). St. Paul exhorts us, "Put on the

---

[38] Hahn, *Catholic Bible Dictionary*, 211.

whole armor of God, that you may be able to stand against the wiles of the devil" (Eph. 6:11). St. Peter tells us, "Be sober, be watchful. Your adversary the devil prowls around like a roaring lion, seeking some one to devour. Resist him, firm in your faith" (1 Pet. 5:8–9). The demons aim fiery darts especially at our faith in Christ (mockery) and at our marriages and families (division).

Church-Approved Arsenal for Resisting Demons

If you are in need of deliverance prayer, may I suggest that you start by making a good sacramental confession? According to Fr. Dennis McManus, a good sacramental confession is more powerful than a thousand exorcisms.[39] Confession is a *sacrament*; exorcism is a *sacramental*. Confession is the powerful step toward healing and deliverance and often takes care of a myriad of demonic ailments. Jesus the Divine Physician lives in the confessor and through him distributes the healing balm of forgiveness.

The following prescription of protection is part of the healing process in the cases in which I have been involved:

+ sacraments: frequent Mass and Confession
+ prayer: Adoration, Liturgy of the Hours, the Rosary, the Chaplet of Divine Mercy
+ Sacred Scripture: *lectio divina*
+ sacramentals: holy water, blessed salt, the Sign of the Cross, the crucifix

---

[39] Fr. McManus stated this as part of a presentation on Confession given to priests in August 2010.

+ enthronement of the Sacred Heart

+ Marian Consecration

+ seven virtues: faith, hope, charity, prudence, justice, temperance, and fortitude

+ deliverance prayers: St. Michael Prayer, St. Patrick's Breastplate, the Magnificat (Luke 1:46–55), the prologue of St. John's Gospel (John 1:1–18), and approved prayers for laity

+ fasting

+ renunciation: renouncing habitual sin, addictions, occult involvement, New Age, witchcraft, Ouija boards, and so forth

+ receiving the Father's blessing (cf. Luke 15:11–32: the parable of the prodigal son)

+ devotion to the angels: St. Michael, your guardian angel, angelic choirs

Divine Mercy for People with Diabolical Suffering

The Church is merciful in the care of God's beloved. Some people are innocent victims of curses, which have the opposite effect of a Christian blessing. If you believe that someone has cursed you or wished you ill, it is helpful to break the curse by praying a blessing upon him or her. It could be a simple prayer such as, "Lord Jesus, if I am a victim of a curse, please protect me and also bless those who wish me ill, and convert their hearts to You, O Lord." In this way you are living the Scripture "Do not return evil for evil or reviling for reviling; but on the contrary bless, for to this you have been called" (1 Pet. 3:9). Curses are too often operative within extended families and mixed cultures. With intentional intercessory prayer, sacrifice, and holiness of life, familial curses are broken.

In desperation some people seek the services of occultists who practice such non-Christian things as divination, that is, trying to predict or control future events, by astrology, Tarot card reading, fortune telling, mediums and psychics, and also by New Age practices such as Reiki Healing Touch. The Church has written an authoritative reflection on *New Age, Jesus Christ: The Bearer of the Water of Life*, which is available online.[40] The commonality here is disordered curiosity and sin against the First Commandment.

Sometimes, although it is difficult for us to fathom, parents who are practicing satanism dedicate their children to Satan. This happens more often than I imagined. Satanism is on the rise globally. Recently, on a major primetime newscast, the anchorwoman interviewed the leader of a satanic temple regarding their legal battle to place a monument to Satan next to the Ten Commandments on the lawn of Oklahoma's State Capitol. Oklahoma opted to remove the Ten Commandments rather than to allow the satanic statue to be placed on state property.[41] The leader of temple later explained that from his childhood he had

---

[40] *Jesus Christ: The Bearer of the Water of Life*: A Christian Reflection on the "New Age," Vatican website, accessed August 21, 2015, http://www.vatican.va/roman_curia/pontifical_councils/interelg/documents/rc_pc_interelg_doc_20030203_new-age_en.html.

[41] Perry Chiaramonte, "Satanic Group Says Oklahoma Must Give the Devil His Due," Fox News, May 5, 2014, accessed July 10, 2015, http://www.foxnews.com/politics/2014/05/05/satanic-group-says-oklahoma-must-give-devil-his-due/.

a fascination with satanism[42] and spoke of the infamous statue as a "counterbalance" to existing religious monuments.[43]

God's mercy plumbs the depths of darkness to rescue people. Eventually many people caught up in the web of evil, after enduring much battering, seek to be set free. They desire to reorient themselves to Jesus Christ. In these cases, Christians and non-Christians seek the Catholic priest. The Holy See asks for increasing prayer for clergy.[44]

Intercessory prayer for priests is vital to the Church's ministry of healing and deliverance, a work of divine mercy.

St. John Chrysostom's Deliverance Prayer
O Eternal God, You who have redeemed the race of men
from the captivity of the Devil, deliver me, Your servant, from
all the workings of unclean spirits. Command the evil and
impure spirits and demons to depart from the soul and body
of Your servant and not to remain nor hide in me. Let them
be banished from me, the creation of Your hands, in Your own
holy name, and that of Your only-begotten Son, and of Your

---

[42] "Lucien Greaves of the Satanic Temple," *Detroit Metro Times*, May 27, 2014, accessed July 10, 2015, http://www.metrotimes.com/detroit/lucien-greaves-of-the-satanic-temple/Content?oid=2201492.

[43] Abby Ohlheiser, "The Satanic Temple's Giant Statue of a Goat-Headed God Is Looking for a Home," *Washington Post*, July 1, 2015, accessed July 10, 2015, http://www.washingtonpost.com/news/acts-of-faith/wp/2015/07/01/the-satanic-temples-giant-statue-of-a-goat-headed-god-is-looking-for-a-home/.

[44] Cf. Congregation for the Clergy, Mauro Cardinal Piacenza, et al., *Eucharistic Adoration for the Sanctification of Priests and Spiritual Maternity* (Roman Catholic Books, 2013), at USCCB website, accessed July 11, 2015, http://www.usccb.org/beliefs-and-teachings/vocations/parents/upload/spiritual-maternity-congregation-fo-clergy.pdf.

life-creating Spirit, so that, after being cleaned from all demonic influence, I may live godly, justly, and righteously and may be counted worthy to receive the Holy Mysteries of Your only-begotten Son and our God, with whom You are blessed and glorified, together with the all-holy and good and life-creating Spirit, now and ever and unto the ages of ages. Amen.[45]

Ordinary Diabolical Activity

At Baptism we renounced Satan and his works. Baptismal grace is dynamic, and we can draw from it throughout our life. Renunciation of everything having to do with evil is necessary. For example, in preparation for Reconciliation, we might pray, "Heavenly Father, in the name of Jesus Christ, I renounce the pornography [or New Age or witchcraft] that I was involved in."

At *every* Mass, prayers are said for healing ("say the word, and my soul shall be healed") and deliverance ("deliver us from evil"). We have the responsibility and spiritual authority to pray prayers of *personal* protection in the form of *deprecative prayer*, that is, prayer seeking to ward off danger or evil by invoking God's power and protection. An example is the prayer to St. Michael the Archangel or St. Patrick's Breastplate. It is very effective to read prayerfully the psalms and the Gospel, as is done during minor and major exorcisms.

Lay faithful are not commissioned to pray *imperative prayer*, that is, a direct command to evil spirits, as this is reserved for ministerial priesthood. This is a matter of proper authority.

---

[45] Quoted in Paul Thigpin, *Manual of Spiritual Warfare* (Charlotte, NC: TAN Books, 2014), 299.

Demons tempt us to the seven capital sins of pride, anger, lust, sloth, envy, greed, and gluttony. The Church Fathers proposed seven virtues to counter the seven capital sins. These include the four cardinal virtues of prudence, justice, temperance, and fortitude and the three theological virtues: faith, hope, and charity.

The *Catechism* lists four ways to *avoid evil*: virtue (CCC 1806), grace (CCC 1889), wisdom (CCC 1950), and the Gospel (CCC 2527).

Common ordinary demonic tactics include pride, deception, accusation, doubt, provocation, diversion, division, and discouragement. Far from a complete list, these are some of the most common diabolical temptations. Satan aims for our most vulnerable sin area and our unhealed wounds.

Extraordinary Demonic Activity

Infestation: demonic activity connected to an object or place, such as a house.

Response: blessing of the property or house with sacramentals by a priest. Your parish pastor is a good place to start, if possible.

Oppression: demonic attacks on a person's exterior life, such as *unusual* family strife, *unusual* persecution at work, or *curious* health issues.

Response: use of Church-approved spiritual weapons; approved prayers of deliverance by the individual; prayers by a priest (need not be the appointed exorcist) and a trained team.

Obsession: severe demonic attacks on a person's interior life, such as inner torment, dreams, temptations to self-destruction.

Response: minor exorcism prayers by the individual, a priest, and a trained team.

Possession: very rare demonic attacks wherein evil spirits periodically control a person's body. Evidenced by very particular manifestation markers.

Response: your bishop's permission is required for major exorcism by the designated exorcist. Usually the priest's name is not made public, and he works with a trained team of laity and priests.

Deliverance Prayer Approved for Laity[46]
My Lord, You are all powerful, You are God, You are Father.
We beg you through the intercession and help of the archangels
Michael, Raphael, and Gabriel for the deliverance of our brothers and sisters who are enslaved by the evil one.
> *From anxiety, sadness, and obsessions,*
> > *we beg You: free us, O Lord.*
> *From hatred, fornication, envy, we beg You:*
> > *free us, O Lord.*
> *From thoughts of jealousy, rage, and death,*
> > *we beg You: free us, O Lord.*
> *From every thought of suicide and abortion,*
> > *we beg You: free us, O Lord.*
> *From every form of sinful sexuality, we beg You:*
> > *free us, O Lord.*
> *From every division in our family, and every harmful*
> > *friendship, we beg You: free us, O Lord.*

---

[46] Bishop Julian Porteous, *Manual of Minor Exorcisms for the Use of Priests* (London: Catholic Truth Society, 2010), 65–66.

*From every sort of spell, malefice, witchcraft, and every
form of the occult, we beg You: free us, O Lord.*

*Lord, You who said, "I leave you peace, my peace I give
you," grant that, through the intercession of the Blessed Virgin
Mary, we may be liberated from every evil spell and enjoy your
peace always. In the name of Jesus Christ, our Lord. Amen.*

Profile in Mercy: St. Maria Faustina Kowalska

God's mercy permeates the Old and New Testaments, but when Jesus desired to emphasize the truth about Divine Mercy for the whole world, He chose a simple Polish nun, Sr. Maria Faustina Kowalska, now known as the Secretary of Divine Mercy.

On February 22, 1931, Jesus appeared to Faustina with rays of blood and water streaming from His Sacred Heart and revealed her special mission to proclaim Divine Mercy to the world: "Write down these words, My daughter, speak to the world about My mercy; let all mankind recognize My unfathomable mercy. It is a sign for end times, after it will come the day of justice. While there is still time, let them have recourse to the fount of My mercy; let them profit from the Blood and Water which gushed forth for them."[1] Much more could be written here, but I will keep with this chapter's theme of spiritual warfare.

St. Faustina's spiritual diary records several occasions of spiritual warfare. "During the night, a soul I had already seen before visited me. However, it did not ask for prayer, but reproached me, saying that I used to be very haughty and vain ... 'and now you are interceding for others while you yourself still have certain vices.' I answered that I indeed had been vain and haughty, but that I had confessed this and had done penance for my stupidity, and that I trusted in the goodness of my God, and if I fell occasionally, this was indeliberate and never premeditated, even in the smallest things. Still, the soul continued to reproach me, saying, 'Why are you unwilling to recognize my greatness? Why do you alone not glorify me for my great deeds as all others do?' Then I saw that this was Satan under the assumed appearance of this soul and I said, 'Glory is due to God alone; begone Satan!' And in an instant this soul fell into an abyss, horrible beyond all description. And I said to the wretched soul that I would tell the whole world about this."[2]

As we know, "Begone, Satan!" is scriptural (Matt. 4:10). We also can repeat these words for ourselves in times of diabolical vexation. The book of Job exemplifies diabolical vexation that many of us experience. Like Job, we are called to persevere until the Lord delivers and restores us.

---

[1] St. Faustina, *Diary*, no. 276.

[2] Ibid., no. 520.

Personal or Group Spiritual Exercise

The Teaching of the Word of God
Read Luke 9:37–43 Jesus Expels the Demon from a Boy.

On the next day, when they had come down from the mountain, a great crowd met him. And behold, a man from the crowd cried, "Teacher, I beg you to look upon my son, for he is my only child; and behold, a spirit seizes him, and he suddenly cries out; it convulses him till he foams, and shatters him, and will hardly leave him. And I begged your disciples to cast it out, but they could not." Jesus answered, "O faithless and perverse generation, how long am I to be with you and bear with you? Bring your son here." While he was coming, the demon tore him and convulsed him. But Jesus rebuked the unclean spirit, and healed the boy, and gave him back to his father. And all were astonished at the majesty of God.

QUESTIONS FOR GROUP OR PERSONAL REFLECTION

1. Jesus answered the father's prayer for the healing and deliverance of his afflicted son. How are you approaching Christ on behalf of your family?

2. In this passage, all were astonished by God's mercy; are you amazed by His mercy in your life?

3. How are you strengthening your spiritual armor (Ephesians 6)?

4. Which of the spiritual weapons are you using to protect yourself and your loved ones?

5. How are you proclaiming Christ's victory over evil in your life and in your family?

Applying God's Mercy

God's Letter to You

My daughter, I want to teach you about spiritual warfare. Never trust in yourself, but abandon yourself totally to My will. In desolation, darkness, and various doubts, have recourse to Me and to your spiritual director. Do not bargain with any temptations; lock yourself immediately in My Heart and, at the first opportunity, reveal the temptation to the confessors. Put your self-love in the last place, so that it does not taint your deeds. Bear with yourself with great patience. Do not neglect interior mortifications. Always justify to yourself the opinions of your superiors and of your confessor. Shun murmurs like a plague. Let all act as they like: you are to act as I want you to. Always fight with the deep conviction that I am with you. Do not be guided by feeling, because it is not always under your control; but all merit lies in the will. I will not delude you with the prospects of peace and consolations; on the contrary, prepare for great battles. Know that you are now on a great stage where all heaven and earth are watching you. Fight like a knight, so that I can reward you. Do not be unduly fearful, because you are not alone.[47]

---

[47] St. Faustina, *Diary*, no. 1767.

Your Letter to God

9

RAYS OF DIVINE MERCY
ON SINNERS AND SAINTS

Healing from Sin-Sickness to the Eucharist

Only Divine Mercy is able to impose limitations on evil;
only the almighty love of God can defeat the tyranny of
the wicked and the destructive power of selfishness and hate.
For this reason, during his last visit to Poland, he said on
his return to the land of his birth: "Apart from the mercy
of God there is no other source of hope for mankind."

—Pope Benedict XVI, Homily on the third anniversary
of the death of Pope John Paul II

A Catholic who seeks inner healing is like a traveler on a journey.
The Holy Spirit helps him to become aware of his heart wound
and mercifully sets him on the road of encounter with Jesus. This
journey is comparable to the situation of the disciples on the road
to Emmaus. On the day of Christ's Resurrection, two men were
walking to the village of Emmaus. They were discussing all the
recent events. They must have been perplexed, their hopes dashed.

IN THIS CHAPTER

+ We will reflect on the Eucharistic healing of the disciples on the road to Emmaus.

+ We will consider God's mercy, inner healing, and knowing yourself in Christ's Eucharistic gaze.

+ We will approach the Eucharist as the fountain of healing mercy.

What were they to make of everything now that Jesus had been crucified? Failure? Then Jesus drew close to them and began to walk and talk with them.

> But their eyes were kept from recognizing him. And he said to them, "What is this conversation which you are holding with each other as you walk?" And they stood still, looking sad....
>
> So they drew near to the village to which they were going. He appeared to be going further, but they constrained him, saying, "Stay with us, for it is toward evening, and the day is now far spent." So he went in to stay with them. When he was at table with them, he took the bread and blessed and broke it, and gave it to them. And their eyes were opened, and they recognized him; and he vanished out of their sight. They said to each other, "Did not our hearts burn within us while he talked to us on the road, while he opened to us the Scriptures?" And they rose that same hour and returned to Jerusalem; and ... told what had happened on the road and how he was known

to them in the breaking of the bread. (Luke 24:13–17, 28–35)

The journey to Eucharistic healing includes many of the emotions experienced by the disciples on the road to Emmaus. We might be perplexed by a circumstance or become profoundly disappointed that what once looked so promising now is ending in failure. There is a breach that wounds our heart. Jesus draws near, but our eyes are kept from recognizing Him. We are in a state of spiritual blindness and deafness. Our understanding is darkened for a time.

Providence will arrange a surprising encounter in which we can see again. Our eyes will be opened in the breaking of the bread. Our heart will begin to burn with love again. The Eucharist rekindles the fire of love to cauterize the bleeding wound. No more thoughts about unknowable mysteries. Jesus makes the mystery beautiful. Bitterness fades. Trust is possible again. Christ absorbs the pain. A new journey begins. "[I]f any one is in Christ, he is a new creation; the old has passed away; behold, the new has come" (2 Cor. 5:17).

Eucharistic Mercy for Inner Healing

In ways seen and unseen the worthy reception of the Eucharist heals sin-sickness. I am one who received inner healing through the sacraments of the Church, especially through my daily Eucharistic life. The need began when the pain of two traumas in my family deeply wounded my heart. By the grace of God I came to understand that because of these two traumas, I lost clarity about my true identity. Once secure as a child of God and experiencing only the love of family and friends into my mid-thirties, two traumas, two years apart, caused me to doubt others and myself. Because of cruel words and deeds, a great spiritual battle ensued between the true and false self. In prayer, an inspiration came, "Take care to heal so that you do not project more wounds upon my Body, the Church." Jesus in the Eucharist became my Divine Physician. At daily Mass and Adoration, divine mercy penetrated my heart wounds, curing the lies of rejection and healing the traumatic memories. Several priests also helped; one personally guided me through the life-changing Spiritual Exercises of St. Ignatius of Loyola for a year. My Magnificat[48] sisters were powerful intercessors also.

Prudence requires that we not overspiritualize inner healing, since Christ also heals communally with health professionals. The Catholic Medical Association[49] is a grounded apostolate that supports the healing ministry of the Church. The Church's healing, deliverance, and exorcism ministry is another way in which Christ heals, and we most often consult with medical professionals. It is not surprising that divine mercy works beautifully through a variety of ways for the care of the beloved. God desires us to be whole and holy.

To Know Yourself in the Gaze of Eucharistic Love

Fr. Jim McManus's Catholic perspective on healing through forgiveness and the need for healthy self-esteem for a life of

---

[48] Magnificat, A Ministry to Catholic Women, based on the Visitation in Luke's Gospel (Luke 1:39–56), is a private association of the faithful with more than a hundred international chapters.

[49] For information on the national and regional work of the Catholic Medical Association, visit its website: www.cathmed.org.

happiness offers good insights.[50] God wills to bring us to a place of joyful, grateful self-acceptance. Fr. McManus calls this a spirituality of true self-esteem wherein we know our true identity as precious children of God. Sometimes we live in the "house of the destructive word," as Fr. Mc Manus terms it. Destructive words impoverish life; hold us back. Constructive words affirm and encourage even when correcting. Healing starts when we move from the "house of the destructive word to the house of the constructive word."[51] There are so many opportunities to build one another up spiritually and emotionally; too often we do the exact opposite. Other people or the devil, or both, tell us lies about ourselves but Abba Father tells us the truth. Nothing separates us from the love of God. Is Christ enough for you?

Having prayed with, listened to, and counseled countless people at international retreats and conferences for twenty years, I have found a common malady in which people struggle with their identity stemming from what they "do" or "have." This is contrary to the Catholic perspective of knowing that we are "temples of the Holy Spirit" (cf. 1 Cor. 6:19). The Eucharist beautifies God's temple.

Fr. McManus understands the separation of psychology and theology, but he sees a synthesis in which our psychological structures relate to our spiritual selves. This challenges core beliefs about the question "Who am I?" Jesus seeks to bring our

---

[50] I find his books helpful, for example: Jim McManus, C.Ss.R., *Healing in the Spirit: Wholeness of Body, Strength of Soul* (Liguori, MO: Liguori Publications, 2002) and *True Self Esteem: Precious in the Eyes of God* (Liguori, MO: Liguori Publications, 2005).

[51] McManus, *Healing in the Spirit*, 22.

self-image into alignment with the truth of divine love. The Eucharist can affect this because by it we are incorporated into Incarnate Truth. When we gaze at the Eucharist in Adoration, Christ mirrors our dignity to us and heals our self-esteem according to the biblical truth of His love.

Eucharistic Healing, Resurrection, the Holy Spirit's Work

In the Eucharist we have direct physical contact with Jesus. This is an important distinction. In the Gospel accounts of people being healed, we discover the fact that everyone who touched Jesus was healed. "[T]hey ... brought to him all that were sick, and begged him that they might only touch the fringe of his garment; and as many as touched it were made well" (Matt. 14:35–36). When we receive the Eucharist, we are touching Jesus, and our communion is physical and spiritual. We touch the Lord as contrite sinners in need of healing medicine and receive Him worthily according to the Church's norms. The sacraments of Confession and Holy Communion are intersecting rivers of divine mercy for healing.

The Eucharist bridges the gap between fallen humanity and redeemed humanity and prepares us for our glorified humanity in Christ's second coming. We are in a process of deification through the Eucharistic life. This process is one of healing from fallen nature (sin) to redeemed nature (sanctity) to glorified nature (transforming union with God: beatific vision). The Holy Spirit is the key agent in the process of transformation in Christ, wherein we are healed. St. Paul often speaks of the Holy Spirit, who mercifully penetrates the areas of our personality that would hold us captive. It is the Holy Spirit who breaks open the mysteries of God's mercy and empowers us to be free. The Holy Spirit brings us to an abiding encounter with Christ in the Eucharist, in which we are grafted like branches onto the vine (cf. John 15:4). This communion is by no means temporary. The physical presence of Christ in the Eucharist is vital because our physicality, our bodies, matter as "temples of the Holy Spirit" (cf. 1 Cor. 6:19).

Healing is resurrection. What was dead is brought to life, what was diseased is restored to health, what was infected is made clean again, what was dormant is awakened. The Eucharist affects your resurrection. Fr. Lawrence Lovasik teaches, "Holy Communion establishes between Jesus Christ and us not merely spiritual contact but physical contact as well through the 'species' of bread. The resurrection of the body can be traced from this physical contact with Christ. The resurrected bodies of those who have worthily received the Eucharist during their lifetime will be more strikingly resplendent because of their frequent contact, during life, with the risen Body of their Lord."[52]

Prayer to Become a Living Monstrance
Lord Jesus, please fashion me into a living Eucharistic monstrance so that I may become a vessel of mercy carrying your love to others. Through our Eucharistic incorporation, grant that I may be a child of the light, salt of the earth, bread for the hungry, water for the thirsty, new wine, and healing oil for others. May people see You in my servant's heart, You in the light of my eyes, in the warmth of my heart, in the works of my

---

[52] Fr. Lawrence G. Lovasik, *The Basic Book of the Eucharist* (Manchester, NH: Sophia Institute Press, 2001), 140.

hands, in the words of my voice, in the incense of my prayer, in the lightness of my laughter, in the glistening of my tears, in the lowliness of your creature. Hide me, I pray, in the gilded monstrance of Your merciful heart so that I will be a living monstrance radiating healing rays of mercy.

Profile in Mercy: St. Maximilian Kolbe

St. Maximilian Kolbe was born Raymond Kolbe in Poland on January 8, 1894, the second of five boys. His childhood was strongly influenced by a vision of Mary in 1906, at the age of twelve. Later he described the incident:

> That night I asked the Mother of God what was to become of me. Then she came to me holding two crowns, one white, the other red. She asked me if I was willing to accept either of these crowns. The white one meant that I should persevere in purity, and the red that I should become a martyr. I said that I would accept them both.[1]

---

[1] Regis J. Armstrong and Ingrid J. Peterson, *The Franciscan Tradition* (Collegeville, MN: Liturgical Press, 2010), 50.

Kolbe and his elder brother Francis joined the Conventual Franciscans in 1907. He professed final vows in 1914, adopting the additional name of Mary. He was sent to Rome and earned doctoral degrees in philosophy and in theology. He was very active in promoting consecration to Mary. On October 16, 1917, Kolbe organized the Knights of the Immaculate One (Militia Immaculata), a movement to work for the conversion of sinners and enemies of the Church, in particular, the Freemasons, whom he saw persecuting the Church in Rome. Love of Mary consumed him. He desired to labor tirelessly to win every heart for Mary.

In 1918, Kolbe was ordained a priest and returned to newly independent Poland in 1919, where he was active in promoting consecration to Mary. Strongly opposed to the communist movement, from 1919 to 1922, he taught at the Kraków seminary. Suffering from tuberculosis forced him to take a lengthy leave of absence from teaching.

In 1927, he established Niepokalanow, the City of the Immaculate, a friary and printing house that eventually grew to one of the largest Franciscan friaries with 762 inhabitants in 1939.

Full of missionary zeal, Maximilian left Poland to journey to the Far East, landing in Nagasaki, Japan, where he and his companions built the Japanese Niepokalanow in the steep slope of Mount Hikosan. In 1945, when the atomic bomb all but leveled Nagasaki, his friary escaped with minimal damage. To this day it is the center of a Franciscan province. In 1939, Maximilian was called back to Poland, where his health deteriorated quickly.

On February17, 1941, he was arrested by the German Gestapo and was imprisoned with four others in the Pawiak Prison. On May 28, 1941, he was sent to Auschwitz and subjected to violent harassment as he continued to act as a priest. He endured beatings and lashings, and on one occasion, his friendly inmates smuggled him to a prison hospital.

In July 1941, after three prisoners disappeared from the camp, the SS deputy camp commander chose ten men to be starved to death in an underground bunker, in order to discourage others from trying to escape. Franciszek Gajowniczek, one of the men selected to die, cried out, "My wife! My children!" and Kolbe volunteered to take his place to spare the life of a husband and father.

An eyewitness testified that Kolbe led the prisoners in prayer to our Lady. After two weeks of dehydration and starvation, the only remaining prisoner was Kolbe. Since the guards wanted to empty the bunker, they gave Kolbe a lethal injection of carbolic acid. Reportedly Kolbe raised his left arm and waited for the deadly injection, which led to his death on August 14, 1941. On the following day, the solemnity of the Assumption of the Blessed Virgin Mary, his remains were cremated.

His Militia of the Immaculata continues to grow and lead souls to Marian Consecration. This priest son of Mary received the crowns that she offered to him in a vision at the tender age of twelve.

Personal or Group Spiritual Exercise

The Teaching of the Word of God
Read Luke 22:14–23: the Last Supper.

And when the hour came, he sat at table, and the apostles with him. And he said to them, "I have earnestly desired to eat this Passover with you before I suffer; for I tell you I shall not eat it until it is fulfilled in the kingdom of God." And he took a chalice, and when he had given thanks he said, "Take this, and divide it among yourselves; for I tell you that from now on I shall not drink of the fruit of the vine until the kingdom of God comes." And he took bread, and when he had given thanks he broke it and gave it to them, saying, "This is my body which is given for you. Do this in remembrance of me." And likewise the chalice after supper, saying, "This chalice which is poured out for you is the new covenant in my blood." But behold the hand of him who betrays me is with me on the table. For the Son of man goes as it has been determined; but woe to that man by whom he is betrayed!" And they began to question one another, which of them it was that would do this.

QUESTIONS FOR GROUP OR PERSONAL REFLECTION

1. As with the disciples on the road to Emmaus, are your eyes being opened at the breaking of the bread? What is Christ trying to show you?

2. Jesus longed for the institution of the Eucharist and the culmination of His mission. How does the Eucharist relate to your vocation?

3. Have you suffered from a wound of betrayal? Prayerfully consider the life lesson learned.

4. Consider Christ's self-emptying love and humility in the Eucharist. How can you become more like Him?

5. Reflect on the healing power of the Precious Blood and how you can bring all people and intentions to this ocean of mercy.

Applying God's Mercy

God's Letter to You
*Look back and count, if you can, all the graces that in My kindness
I have given you. When you still were not, I had your name written
in My heart. Many others would have served and loved Me better
than you, but I had chosen you from all eternity. And I rejoiced in
giving you being, in impregnating you with graces, in preparing you,
through the Eucharistic banquet, a cross as a precious gift of My
affection.*

*I knew that your parents would die; I would not leave you
orphans. When they died they left goods, but they could not leave
themselves. I can because I am all powerful and infinite, and more
loving than all parents. I give you My Body, Soul, and Divinity.*

Eat today this infinite Good because I only want now to be one with you. "My flesh is real food and My Blood real drink. The man who eats My flesh and drinks My Blood remains in Me and I in him" (John 6:55–56).

I came into the world to be close to you. . . . That is why I suffered and died on the Cross to purchase for you the joys of reconciliation, to give you sacraments and in them My Heart to cleanse you from your sins. Therefore, finally, I am here in the Eucharist, as a miracle of omnipotence, hiding My splendor to adjust to the material of your heart. You may lack in the world hearts that love you, but not Mine! You will always have Me on the altars, ready to wipe your tears, to listen to your confidences, to take My Heart from My bosom and place it into yours. Open your heart with humility, yes, but with holy enthusiasm. I have come to fill you in the most intimate part of your being. Come, come, close![53]

Your Letter to God

---

[53] Venerable Concepción Cabrera de Armida, *I AM: Eucharistic Meditations on the Gospel* (New York: Society of St. Paul, 2001), 62–63.

10

RAYS OF DIVINE MERCY ON MARRIAGE

Healing from Spiritual Weakness to the Beatitudes

*Merciful love is supremely indispensable between those who
are closest to one another: between husbands and wives,
between parents and children, between friends; and it is
indispensable in education and in pastoral work.*

—Pope John Paul II, *Dives in Misericordia*

The book of Tobit eloquently reminds us that the sacrament of
marriage is a love story with God in the middle.

"When the door was shut and the two were alone, Tobias
got up from the bed and said, 'Sister, get up, and let us pray
and implore our Lord that he grant us mercy and safety.'
And they began to say,
'Blessed are you, O God of our fathers,
 and blessed be your holy and glorious name for ever.
 Let the heavens and all your creatures bless you.

You made Adam and gave him Eve his wife as a helper
and support.
From them the race of mankind has sprung.
You said, "It is not good that the man should be alone;
let us make a helper for him like himself."
And now, O Lord, I am not taking this sister of mine
because of lust, but with sincerity. Grant that I may find
mercy and may grow old together with her.' And they
both said, 'Amen, amen.'" (Tob. 8:4–8)

Again we cry out to God, "Call down your mercy on marriage!" We are called to exercise our prophetic voice to protect
the sublime authenticity of sacramental marriage. The inspired
book of Tobit is a striking reflection on God's mercy and an
important reminder that when God is in the middle of marriage,
spouses are healed, delivered, and blessed. Marriage, elevated to
a sacramental state, is a priceless gift to couples, children, society,
and Church. The "merciful love" that St. John Paul II speaks of
in his encyclical *Dives in Misericordia* is indispensable to the vital-
ity of marriage as God envisioned it. Pope John Paul II recognized
that sacramental marriage and matters relating to sex, the body,
and the family are the battleground of the war between good and
evil, and he gave us the gift of the Theology of the Body.[54]

Healing the Wounds of Marriage

On June 24, 2015, in his general audience in Rome, Pope Francis
preached on the wounds of the family:

---

[54] John Paul II's Theology of the Body is his magnum opus on the human
person, written between 1979 and 1984 as a series of reflections. See
https://www.ewtn.com/library/PAPALDOC/JP2TBIND.HTM.

IN THIS CHAPTER

+ We will reflect on healing the wounds of marriage through the medicine of merciful love.

+ We will consider marriage in God's plan, marriage in the regime of sin, and eight healthful habits for couples.

+ We will reflect on ways to heal and strengthen marriage through the Beatitudes.

We know well that every family on occasion suffers moments when one family member offends another. The resulting wounds come from words, actions and omissions, which, instead of expressing love, hurt those nearest and dearest, causing deep divisions among family members, above all between husband and wife. If these wounds are not healed in time, they worsen and turn into resentment and hostility, which then fall to the children. When the wounds are particularly deep they can even lead a spouse to search for understanding elsewhere, to the detriment of the family.

We have a responsibility to God and to one another to apply medicinal mercy wherever there is a wound. Probably we have experienced the deep fissures of the heart wounded by marital and family divisions that beg for healing.

I was struck by additional comments of the Supreme Pontiff during the same Wednesday audience: "We speak a lot about behavioral problems, mental health, the well-being of the child, the anxiety of the parents and the children—but do we even know what a wound of the soul is? Do we feel the weight of the mountain that crushes the soul of a child in those families where members mistreat and hurt one another to the point of breaking the bonds of marital fidelity? What effect do our choices—often poor choices—have on the souls of children?" he asked. The pope concluded with a prayer for "a deep love to approach all families with His merciful heart."[55]

Do we sense the eagerness of God to open the floodgates of mercy to heal marriages? Believers have a grave responsibility to engage in the spiritual war to reclaim marriage according to God's original plan in the ordered harmony of Eden, when He created us male and female.

Sacramental marriage, unsupported by the present anti-Christian culture, requires graced due diligence. There was a time when my marriage nearly unraveled. The emotional wounds came from within and without. *Forgiveness saved us.* I thank God for calling my husband and me into the vocation of sacramental marriage and for blessing us with the undeserved gift of children. We made mistakes and yet are held together by the amazing grace of the sacrament. Through prayerful discernment, the grace came to understand that marriage is too precious a gift of God to discard. The sacrifice is beautiful when understood in the light of the dignity of marriage that reflects the spousal love of God for His Church. Marriage, worth every effort, is one of the greatest goods of divine mercy.

Absent God in the middle, marriage according to His plan is nearly impossible in our secular culture, where anything goes. Marriage challenges our selfishness, egoism, independence, and

---

[55] Pope Francis, general audience, June 24, 2015.

indulgence. Ideally marriage is where the male and female hearts intertwine with the merciful heart of the Redeemer to produce more charity.

Family built on the solid foundation of a happy marriage is happening less today for a number of reasons. William B. May, President of Catholics for the Common Good and author of *Getting the Marriage Conversation Right*,[56] says that although a high percentage of high school seniors still aspire to marriage, "the numbers achieving their dreams of marriage has dropped precipitously. Marriage is in crisis." For children the stakes are extremely high. Anyone who, as a child, has suffered his parents' divorce can attest to this. In my family, when a cousin divorced, his son committed suicide. Such wounds beg God's mercy. The Church is on the forefront of defending marriage and family in the public square; this is a mission for all the faithful.

Later in this chapter, I propose the Beatitudes as a way of strengthening marriages. Here I paraphrase Dr. Gregory Popcak's eight marriage-friendly habits that many happy married couples exhibit as presented in *When Divorce Is Not an Option*.[57] Please do not become demoralized if your marriage is missing these habits. Pray and discern whether these might be helpful and patiently begin.

+ "Rituals of Connection": work, play, talk, prayer

+ "Emotional Rapport and Benevolence": Gal. 6:2: "bear one another's burdens"

---

[56] William B. May, *Getting the Marriage Conversation Right* (Steubenville, OH: Emmaus Road Publishing, 2012), 2.

[57] Dr. Gregory K. Popcak, *When Divorce Is Not an Option* (Manchester, NH, Sophia Institute Press, 2014), 54.

+ "Self-regulation": capacity to stay calm and to regain composure even under pressure.

+ "A Positive Intention Frame": the ability to assume the best about your spouse even at his or her worst.

+ "Caretaking in Conflict": solving the problem is not as important as taking care of each other as you work toward the solution.

+ "Mutual Respect, Accountability, and Boundaries": Ephesians 5:21 challenges husbands and wives to defer to one another out of reverence for Christ.

+ "Reviewing and Learning from Mistakes": work hard to learn from mistakes and do not dredge up past hurts or attack each other. But do not ignore the past so that mistakes are not repeated.

+ "Getting Good Support": choose wisely your network of support: friends, family, pastors, and counselors.[58]

Marriage in God's Plan

It may be helpful to consider the following in light of the virtues: chastity, temperance, charity, diligence, patience, kindness, and humility.

The matrimonial covenant, by which a man and a woman establish between themselves a partnership of the whole of life, is by its nature ordered toward the good of the spouses and the procreation and education

---

[58] Popcak, *When Divorce Is Not an Option*, 81.

of offspring; this covenant between baptized persons has been raised by Christ the Lord to the dignity of a sacrament.

Sacred Scripture begins with the creation of man and woman in the image and likeness of God and concludes with a vision of "the wedding-feast of the Lamb." Scripture speaks throughout of marriage and its "mystery," its institution and the meaning God has given it, its origin and its end, its various realizations throughout the history of salvation, the difficulties arising from sin and its renewal "in the Lord" in the New Covenant of Christ and the Church. (CCC 1601–1602)

Marriage Under the Regime of Sin

It may be helpful to consider the following in light of the capital sins: pride, lust, gluttony, greed, sloth, anger, and envy.

Every man experiences evil around him and within himself. This experience makes itself felt in the relationships between man and woman. Their union has always been threatened by discord, a spirit of domination, infidelity, jealousy, and conflicts that can escalate into hatred and separation. This disorder can manifest itself more or less acutely, and can be more or less overcome according to the circumstances of cultures, eras, and individuals, but it does seem to have a universal character. (CCC 1606)

According to faith the disorder we notice so painfully does not stem from the *nature* of man and woman, nor from the nature of their relations, but from sin. As a break with God, the first sin had for its first consequence the rupture of the original communion between man and woman. Their relations were distorted by mutual recriminations; their mutual attraction, the Creator's own gift, changed into a relationship of domination and lust; and the beautiful vocation of man and woman to be fruitful, multiply, and subdue the earth was burdened by the pain of childbirth and the toil of work (CCC 1607).

Prayer for Marriage:
Ever More a Woman, Ever More a Man
Most Holy Trinity, we come before you as husband and wife
bound in the sacrament of matrimony by chords of divine
love. You called us to this sacrament of communion assuring
us of your presence, grace, and protection. We are sorry for
our mutual imperfection of love, weakness in virtue, taking
each other for granted, hurtful actions and words, insecuri-
ties and indiscretions. We ask you to restore us, to renew
what we have lost, to heal what has been wounded and worn
out. Graciously restore our joy of journeying together through
the adventure of life with you in the middle of our hearts. As
spouses we entrust ourselves to your merciful love that heals
all wounds. Grant a drop of your Precious Blood to fall upon
us now. We echo the words of Christ's Vicar, "I love you, and
for this love I help you to become ever more a woman"; "I love
you, and for this love I help you to become ever more a man."
Jesus, we trust in You.[59]

---

[59] Within the quotation are selections from Pope Francis's homily at the Mass for the Rite of Marriage, St. Peter's Square, September 14, 2014.

The Beatitudes Strengthen Marriages

Christ preached the eight Beatitudes (Matt. 5:1–12) in His Sermon on the Mount. The Beatitudes present a spirituality of *humility*. It's sometimes hard to know how to live humility. The Beatitudes can strengthen a couple in the art of merciful love.

"Blessed are the poor in spirit, for theirs is the kingdom of heaven."

Lord Jesus, in our marriage, help us to embrace spiritual poverty willingly. Grant that we keep our hearts set on heaven and not expect paradise on earth.

"Blessed are those who mourn, for they shall be comforted."

Lord Jesus, assist us in our times of grief and sorrow with Your comforting embrace and healing mercy.

"Blessed are the meek, for they shall inherit the earth."

Lord Jesus, graciously help us in our marriage to cultivate gentle, servants' hearts and meekness that does not admit of the building of walls.

"Blessed are those who hunger and thirst for righteousness, for they shall be satisfied."

Lord Jesus, grant that we may thirst for righteousness, authenticity, and justice while incorporating merciful love into our daily lives.

"Blessed are the merciful, for they shall obtain mercy."

Lord Jesus, we pray to be always merciful in our marriage, in word and deed, striving to be vessels of mercy for each other first.

"Blessed are the pure in heart, for they shall see God."

> *Lord Jesus, we pray for pure hearts, unsullied bodies, and a holy thought life. Please heal us of wounds of impurity that could impact our marriage.*

"Blessed are the peacemakers, for they shall be called sons of God."

> *Lord Jesus, graciously make us authentic peacemakers in our marriage — not afraid of having the difficult conversations we need to have, but trusting that we can dialogue in gentle truth.*

"Blessed are those who are persecuted for righteousness' sake, for theirs is the kingdom of heaven."

> *Lord Jesus, strengthen us in our marriage when we undergo persecution for the sake of justice. Help us not to back down from our Catholic Faith, mindful of Your grace, which is always sufficient.*

Profile in Mercy: Venerable (Conchita) Concepción Cabrera de Armida

Conchita was a wife and mother of nine children who lived during one of the most turbulent times in Mexican history—an age of religious persecution, revolution, and economic depression. Her spirituality developed through the intimate interaction of love for her husband, her children, and Christ and His Church.

Her son Manuel was ordained a Jesuit priest in 1922. Thirty-three-year-old Manuel wrote to his mother before his ordination day, "Mother, I put everything back into your hands, just as when you held me to your chest as a very small child, teaching me the beautiful names of Jesus and Mary, and introducing me to this mystery. I really feel like an infant asking for your light, your prayer and your sacrifice.... As soon as I am a priest, I will send you my blessing, and then I will receive yours on my knees."[1]

Over the course of many years, Jesus prepared Conchita to live a Eucharistic life of spiritual motherhood for priests. Jesus once explained to her, "There are souls who through ordination receive a priestly anointing. However, there are ... also priestly souls who do not have the dignity of or the ordination of a priest, yet have a priestly mission. They offer themselves united to me.... These souls help the Church in a very powerful spiritual way.... You will be the mother of a great number of spiritual children, yet they will cost your heart the death of a

---

[1] Congregation for the Clergy, Mauro Cardinal Piacenza, et al., *Eucharistic Adoration for the Sanctification of Priests and Spiritual Maternity,* 25.

thousand martyrs."[2] She became a vessel of divine mercy for countless priests.

Venerable Conchita is featured in my book *Praying for Priests: A Mission for the New Evangelization* and is a patron for the Foundation of Prayer for Priests.[3] Some half a million copies of her spiritual writings on the Eucharist and the priesthood were distributed during her lifetime and today continue to enflame hearts with the love of Jesus. Christ once told her, "Do not fear.... If up until now you have been unfaithful ... ungrateful ... a sinner and less gentle with Me. See, I am the Lamb of God Who takes away the sins of the world.... It is for this that My Precious Blood is daily at your disposal, so that you can drink it ... so you may purify yourself ... so you may become holy receiving My Divinity, its substance which is purity itself. Do not fear!"

Her cause for beatification is under way. The Congregation for the Clergy wrote of Conchita, "In the future, she will be of great importance for the universal Church." A wife, mother, widow, and foundress, a contemplative in action, Venerable Conchita illustrates the feminine genius of receptivity for God and Church.

---

[2] Congregation for the Clergy, Mauro Cardinal Piacenza, et al., *Eucharistic Adoration for the Sanctification of Priests and Spiritual Maternity*, 24.

[3] See under Learn More: Our Patrons: Spiritual Motherhood, Foundation of Prayer for Priests, www.foundationforpriests.org.

Personal or Group Spiritual Exercise

The Teaching of the Word of God
Read Matthew 5:1–12: the Sermon on the Mount.

Seeing the crowds, he went up on the mountain, and when he sat down his disciples came to him. And he opened his mouth and taught them, saying:

"Blessed are the poor in spirit, for theirs is the kingdom of heaven.

"Blessed are those who mourn, for they shall be comforted.

"Blessed are the meek, for they shall inherit the earth.

"Blessed are those who hunger and thirst for righteousness, for they shall be satisfied.

"Blessed are the merciful, for they shall obtain mercy.

"Blessed are the pure in heart, for they shall see God.

"Blessed are the peacemakers, for they shall be called sons of God.

"Blessed are those who are persecuted for righteousness' sake, for theirs is the kingdom of heaven.

"Blessed are you when men revile you and persecute you and utter all kinds of evil against you falsely on my account. Rejoice and be glad, for your reward is great in heaven, for so men persecuted the prophets who were before you."

QUESTIONS FOR GROUP OR PERSONAL REFLECTION

1. Are you presently living the Beatitudes, and if so, how are you benefitting?

2. Which beatitude do you find most difficult to live in your daily life, and why?

3. Is there a marriage wound from the past or present that needs God's medicine of mercy? Pray and discern how to apply merciful love for healing.

4. Are you and your spouse willing to pray together for any necessary healing and to forgive one another everything?

5. Would your marriage benefit from a visit to your parish priest to ask his prayer and blessing on your marriage?

6. For single people, if you feel called to marriage, are you intentionally praying for God to choose your spouse?

Applying God's Mercy

God's Letter to You
Once again, then, I urge you to have even greater confidence in God, for it is written that those who trust in Him will never be forsaken (cf. Sir 2:10). Don't turn in on yourself as so often

happens, unfortunately. In the midst of the trials which may afflict you, just place all your confidence in our Supreme Good in the knowledge that He takes more care of us than a mother takes of her child (cf. Sir 4:10). Don't allow any sadness to dwell in your soul, for sadness prevents the Holy Spirit from acting freely. If we insist on being sad, then let it be a holy sadness at the sight of the evil that is spreading more and more in society nowadays. How many poor souls are every day deserting God, our Supreme Good! To refuse to submit one's own judgment to that of others, especially to those who are quite expert in the field in question, is a sign that we possess very little docility and an all too obvious sign of secret pride. You know this yourself and you agree with me. Well, then, take heart and avoid falling into this fault again. Keep your eyes open for this wretched vice, knowing how much it displeased Jesus, for it is written that God opposes the proud, but gives grace to the humble.[60]

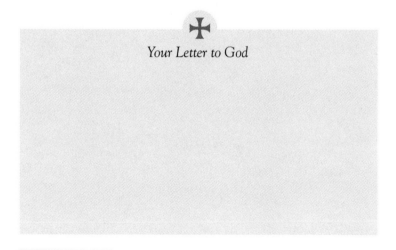

Your Letter to God

---

[60] St. Padre Pio of Pietrelcina, *Letters Vol. II, Correspondence with Raffaelina Cerase, Noblewoman 1914–1915* (Foggia, Italy: Our Lady of Grace Friary, 1987), 260.

11

RAYS OF DIVINE MERCY ON THE UNBORN, THE ELDERLY, AND CHILDREN

Healing from Worldliness to Works of Mercy

In the parables devoted to mercy, Jesus reveals the nature of God as that of a Father who never gives up until he has forgiven the wrong and overcome rejection with compassion and mercy.

—Pope Francis, Bull of Indiction of the
Extraordinary Jubilee of Mercy, 9

Several years ago I led a retreat on divine mercy for the young adults at St. Stanislaus Kostka Parish in the Archdiocese of Chicago. The parish opened in 1867 and was enlarged to accommodate the immense flow of Polish immigrants into the neighborhood. In 2007, Cardinal Francis George designated the parish as the Sanctuary of the Divine Mercy in Chicago. In 2008, he blessed the iconic monstrance, Our Lady of the Sign–Ark of Mercy, which draws many people to Eucharistic Adoration.

IN THIS CHAPTER

+ We will reflect on healing mercy for the unborn, the elderly, and children.

+ We will consider children's need to be formed in the spirituality of merciful love.

+ We will consider how prayer energizes the works of mercy.

The Marian monstrance is truly outstanding for its scale and profound theological witness of Mary, Mother of the Eucharist and of Mercy.

The polar opposite of this beautiful Marian Eucharistic spirituality is the narcissistic spirituality of worldliness. An example is when Catholics use the Church for their spiritual comfort while rejecting her teachings at their will. Such people are in need of conversion and healing, which can occur through God's mercy. Intercessory prayer can transform worldliness to works of mercy necessary for the unborn, the elderly, and children.

Living Mercy for the Unborn and the Elderly

After I gave a Friday-night conference in Chicago, the parishioners invited me to pray in front of the Planned Parenthood abortion clinic on Division Street, not far from the parish. On Saturday morning my host drove to the abortion clinic, and we joined many young families in praying the Rosary at 7 a.m. There were several couples with babies in strollers and mothers who were pregnant. It was an impressive, well-organized pro-life scene. I was handed a large pro-life poster and took my place in the line along Division Street. Many cars honked, one cab driver yelled, "My mom is pro-life—she had ten kids!" Other drivers were less than kind, and many hand gestures were directed at us.

Several young mothers walked into that abortion clinic but not without being offered some loving pro-life truth and materials amid the gentle rhythm of the Rosary prayers. One worker came out of the clinic and yelled at me, "Why are you here? You are making it harder for these women to do what they need to do! You make things worse for these poor women." I thought to myself, "What a lie!" They do not have to abort their baby; there are better alternatives, and we can help.

Then I was drawn to a car parked outside the abortion clinic because a young man in the driver's seat was weeping. His window was down, so I gently approached him. "Are you all right? Can I help you?" The emotional young man could barely speak. His girlfriend was inside the clinic, and they would not let him enter because he did not want his baby to be aborted. He wanted to keep the baby, but he wasn't given a choice. He was shaken to the core. Where's the mercy in this situation?

On the other end of the spectrum, my maternal grandmother, afflicted with Alzheimer's disease in her late seventies, was in a nursing home for six years, bedridden and in the fetal position, eventually unable to recognize her family. After six years, a battle between family members and medical caregivers ensued regarding whether to cease nutrition. She was not on life support and was able to take food, but some nursing-home staff suggested that she not be fed. They offered the family this option as an act of mercy to hasten the inevitable.

The attitude of the nursing-home staff in the case of my grandmother and the attitude of the abortion-clinic worker reflect an attitude of spiritual worldliness. Fr. John Hardon defines *worldliness* as "the mental attitude of a person who is guided by secular ideas rather than by religious principles, and whose primary concern is for well-being in this life and not in the life to come."[61]

God's mercy is not about killing the unborn or the elderly, although with secular mentality, doing so is touted as merciful. The culture of death is not without demonic influence since we opened doors legislatively to welcome the prince of death. The world is full of evil because of our free will. God offers true healing, true mercy, to all in need of healing. Post-abortive women have received healing mercy in apostolates such as Rachel's Vineyard.[62] God is infinitely forgiving, as seen in the parable of the woman caught in adultery.

Divine Mercy for Children

Children are most vulnerable in today's anti-Christian culture of death with broken families and marriages. At the Napa Institute last year I heard lectures concerning the lack of children in years to come and the adjustment the Church will need to make. This challenging situation beckons the faithful to heroic virtue in the responsibility of parenting children in the truths of the Faith. Here are suggestions drawn from Fr. Lawrence

---

[61] Hardon, *Modern Catholic Dictionary.*

[62] For more information about Rachel Vineyard: see www.rachelsvineyard. org.

Lovasik's *Catholic Family Handbook*[63] to help form children in merciful love.

+ "Know your duties as a parent." Prioritize parental duties according to God's law of mercy for men, women, and children.

+ "Use your God-given authority to guide your children." Understand and exercise your parental authority as a duty, a privilege, and a joy for the security of your children and for order in your home.

+ "Help develop your children's personality." The discovery of a child's unique personality is a surprising adventure and honor that allows parents to be cooperators with divine grace.

+ "Teach your children good manners." A polite, well-mannered child is a treasure. Teaching proper etiquette in different social settings enriches the child, the family, and the culture.

+ "Raise your children in the Faith." The parental privilege for the spiritual formation of children is a gift and a responsibility entrusted by God. Praying with children, an act of mercy, is vital for their wellness and protection.

+ "Learn how to prevent misbehavior." Lead by the example of good behavior. Communication is an act of merciful love.

+ "Learn how to deal with misbehavior." Respond with consistency, patience, prayer, responsibility and forgiveness.

---

[63] Lawrence G. Lovasik, *The Catholic Family Handbook* (Manchester, NH, Sophia Institute Press, 2000), 101.

+ "Use punishment prudently." Accountability is important, but so is the loving care of young, impressionable minds and hearts.

+ "Discipline your teenagers wisely." Consistency, communication, and accountability teach teenagers to be responsible to themselves and others.

+ "Foster love in your home and family." Mindful of the Holy Family in Nazareth, create a home atmosphere of peace, joy, prayer, and merciful love.

Prayer Energizes the Works of Mercy

For Catholics, prayer is life. For a time in the early years of my marriage, I ceased daily prayer to the detriment of my family and myself. It was Mary who never ceased to prompt me to resume my prayer life. Prayer is a wellspring of grace. Fr. Tadeusz Dajczer explains.

> You are as much a Christian as you are capable of praying. Prayer and its particular stages are signs and indication of your closeness to or distance from God. Everything depends on God; it is He who decides and only He can give you strength. The tragedy of our Christian activism is that activities really do smother us. The more suppressed you are with activities, the more time you should dedicate to prayer. Otherwise you will be empty; you will have the impression that you are giving something but this will be only an illusion. You cannot give that which you do not have.[64]

---

[64] Fr. Tadeusz Dajczer, *The Gift of Faith* (Newark, NJ: Families of Nazareth Movement Publishing, 2000), 195.

Most people are buried in activities, and this is why we should pray more, not less. At a retreat, I was encouraging people to get in the habit of making a daily holy hour. A woman commented that she didn't think it was possible for mothers to pray an hour daily. A homeschooling mother of eight children responded that she arises an hour before the family to make her holy hour. She tells her children that for her to be the best possible mother and wife, she gives the first hour of her day to God. What a beautiful witness! Time spent in prayer with the Divine Mercy energizes us for the family and the works of mercy. What is more important than God in your life?

Healing Mercy for Family

When our second son was in high school, he was diagnosed (by blood test) with mononucleosis and was told by doctors to stay in bed for two months. This meant that he would not graduate with his class. This news was devastating for him. After returning home from the doctor's office, he took to his bed as ordered.

A priest friend, who joined us for dinner that evening, suggested that we pray with my son, that he might be healed. I appreciated Father's idea, but I didn't expect a healing. After dinner, we proceeded to my son's room and asked if he would like Father to bless him. He agreed. Father said, "Kathleen, you love your son very much. Your prayer will be most powerful. Why don't you ask God to heal your son now?" We each said a prayer asking God to be merciful and heal him so that he could graduate with his class. While I was making coffee in the kitchen the next morning, my son appeared dressed for school, saying, "Mom, I feel fine. I can go to school." I checked his vital signs, and they were normal. This healing meant the world to my son. God is not only kind and merciful but practical also. It never hurts to pray for the healing we desire. God expects us to ask. Sometimes the healing may be delayed, or it may be God's will *not to heal* because He has a better plan. In faith, we place no limit on the mercy of God. Ask for healing! God will respond by saying "yes," or "not yet," or "I have a better plan."

Profile in Mercy: St. Gianna Beretta Molla

Born in Milan, Italy, on October 4, 1922, the tenth of thirteen children, St. Gianna, as a young girl, exhibited a strong gift of faith and understood the necessity and effectiveness of prayer. Her excellent parents provided a solid Christian education, and she dedicated herself to studies from primary school through university education. She also applied her faith in apostolic service among the elderly and the needy as a member of the St. Vincent de Paul Society.

In 1949, after earning her medical degree from the University of Pavia, she opened a medical clinic near Magenta in 1950. At the University of Milan in 1952 she specialized in pediatrics and continued to give special attention to mothers, babies, the poor, and the elderly.

Gianna considered working in the medical field as a mission. She contributed generously to Catholic Action, especially among the very young. Vivacious with a love for God's creation, she enjoyed skiing and mountaineering. She often reflected on the God-given gift of her vocation as a physician.

Called to the vocation of marriage, Gianna enthusiastically embraced it. She dedicated herself to forming a Christian family, pleasing to God. She married Pietro Molla on September 24, 1955, in St. Martin's Basilica in Magenta. A very happy wife, to her joy, she became the mother to Pierluigi in November 1956; to Mariolina in December 1957, and to Laura in July 1959. She was able to blend the demands of mother, wife, and doctor and her passion for life with simplicity and zest.

In September 1961, toward the end of the second month of another pregnancy, she was touched by suffering and the mystery of pain; she had developed a fibroma in her uterus. Before the required surgical operation, and conscious of the risk that her continued pregnancy brought, she pleaded with the surgeon to save the life of the child she was carrying, and entrusted herself to prayer and providence. The baby's life was saved, for which she thanked the Lord. She spent the seven months remaining until the birth of the child in incomparable strength of spirit and unrelenting dedication to her tasks as mother and doctor.

A few days before the child was due, although trusting as always in providence, she was ready to give her life in order to save that of her child: "If you must decide between me and the child, do not hesitate: choose the child—I insist on it. Save the baby." On the morning of April 21, 1962, Gianna Emanuela was born. Despite all efforts and treatments to save both of them, on the morning of April 28, 1962, amid unspeakable pain and after repeated exclamations of "Jesus, I love you. Jesus, I love you," the mother died. She was thirty-nine years old. Her funeral was an occasion of profound grief, faith, and prayer. Gianna was canonized on May 16, 2004.[1]

The miracle needed for Gianna's canonization is as follows: in 2000, Elisabeth Comparini Arcolino, a mother of three, at sixteen weeks pregnant with her fourth child, sustained a tear in the placenta; this resulted in the loss of her amniotic fluid. She was told that the baby would not survive. By divine providence, Bishop Diogenes Silva Matthes of Franca, Brazil, was at the hospital visiting a friend. He was summoned to Arcolino's room, and she told him that the doctor had advised her to have an abortion. "You don't kill life inside the mother," the bishop replied. "This is the time for St. Gianna Beretta Molla to intercede for the life you are carrying."

At home the bishop prayed to St. Gianna, "The time for your canonization has arrived. Intercede to the Lord for the grace of a miracle and save the life of this little baby." Despite the lack of amniotic fluid, Elisabeth

---

[1] See Gianna Beretta Molla website, accessed June 26, 2015, http://saintgianna.org/main.htm.

delivered a healthy girl, Gianna Maria, by caesarean section on May 31, 2000. The Arcolino family was present for the canonization, as were Gianna's husband and three children.[2] St. Gianna is a patron for mothers, physicians, and unborn children.

[2] "Path to Canonization," Saint Gianna Beretta Molla website, accessed August 21, 2015, http://saintgianna.org/stgiannascannonization.htm.

Group or Personal Retreat Exercise

The Teaching of the Word of God
Read Matthew 25:35–40: The Corporal Works of Mercy.

1. Feed the hungry: "I was hungry and you gave me food."

2. Give drink to the thirsty: "I was thirsty and you gave me drink."

3. Clothe the naked: "I was naked and you clothed me."

4. Shelter the homeless: "I was a stranger and you welcomed me."

5. Visit the sick: "I was sick and you visited me."

6. Visit the imprisoned: "I was in prison and you came to me."

7. Bury the dead: "Truly, I say to you, as you did it to one of the least of these my brethren, you did it to me."

QUESTIONS FOR GROUP OR
PERSONAL REFLECTION

1. Reflect on the Corporal Works of Mercy. Did you ever count on someone else's mercy for you?

2. Think of the times when you engaged in doing a corporal work of mercy. What was that encounter like?

3. In light of the pro-life reflection in this chapter, do you have a wound that needs God's merciful love?

4. Jesus invites us to reach out to those in need of mercy. Are the works of mercy part of your life?

5. What would you consider God's greatest act of mercy for you personally? Give thanks and praise to God. How can you become more of a vessel of mercy for others?

Applying God's Mercy

God's Letter to You
My child, you are never secure in this life. As long as you live you will always need spiritual weapons. You are in the midst of enemies, who may attack from the right hand or left. If you do not make use of the shield of patience on all occasions, it is certain you will

be wounded before long. Moreover, if you do not fix your heart on Me, with the sincere will to endure all things for My sake, you will be unable to stand under the heat of battle and will fail to win the palm I reserve for My saints. Therefore, you must bear all courageously, using a strong hand against all that stands in your way. The person who overcomes is fed with the Bread of heaven but to the coward is left much misery. If you rest in this life, how can you expect to deserve eternal rest? True peace is found only in heaven, not in the human person or any other creature, but in God alone. You must be willing to suffer all things gladly for the love of God: labors, sorrows, temptations, afflictions; all anxieties, needs, infirmities, injuries, detraction, rebukes; all humiliations, confusions, corrections, and contempt. Such things are aids in virtue and test those for a heavenly crown. For this short labor I will give an eternal reward, and for passing confusion, infinite glory.[65]

Your Letter to God

---

[65] Thomas à Kempis, *The Imitation of Christ*, 189.

12

RAYS OF DIVINE MERCY ON THE WHOLE WORLD

Healing the Culture through the Spiritual Works of Mercy

*May all that the Church says and does manifest the mercy
God feels for man, and therefore for us. From Divine Mercy,
which brings peace to hearts, genuine peace flows into the
world, peace between different peoples, cultures and religions.*

—Pope Benedict XVI, Regina Caeli Message, March 30, 2008

Jesus Christ is the face of the Father's mercy that we long to
see. Whenever we truly encounter the face of the Divine Mercy,
we are healed at some level; we become more Christ-like from
within. Before we engage in the Spiritual or Corporal Works of
Mercy, to distinguish ourselves from secular nonbelievers who
engage in worthy charities also, our Catholic heart should radiate something profoundly different. The difference is a sense
of humility that we have been the unworthy recipients of the
mercy of God, who has loved us first. We are merely servants of
the Divine Mercy.

IN THIS CHAPTER

+ We will reflect on the face of healing mercy.
+ We will consider the Spiritual Works of Mercy and their power to heal.
+ We will consider how works of mercy heal and protect the culture.

One person in particular revealed the face of the Father's mercy to me: Karol Wojtyla. Whether I saw him in Rome or read his writings or watched him on television, he radiated God's mercy for me. He struck a precise chord in my heart that released in me a greater love for God and His Church. This is the power of the face of God's mercy. It is difficult to articulate such an intimate human reaction of the heart. More than once while speaking at various conferences, I found myself becoming quite emotional when speaking of him. As I was giving a conference in Trinidad, at the mention of St. John Paul II, not only did I get choked up, but most of the people in attendance wept as well. Human emotions arise when the face of the Divine Mercy is manifest.

Believers desire and desperately need to encounter the living, joyful, truthful, majestic face of the Father of Mercy—healer and lover of humanity.

Healing Miraculous Mercy

According to Msgr. Slawomir Oder, postulator of the Polish pontiff's cause of beatification, he was "a man who lived in the presence of God, who let himself be guided by the Holy Spirit, who was in constant dialogue with the Lord, and who built his whole life around the question [asked of Peter]: 'Do you love me?' "[66]

During the diocesan process, approximately 130 testimonies of healing were heard. Mercy heals!

The Vatican recognized Sr. Marie Simon-Pierre's testimony of healing from Parkinson's disease written in 2006 as a miracle attributed to the intercession of John Paul II. Sister reported, "It feels as if I have been reborn." In her words, the story of a miracle:

> In June 2001, I was diagnosed with Parkinson's disease.... After three years, the initial phase of the disease, slow, but progressive, was followed by an aggravation of the symptoms: accentuation of the trembling, rigidity, pain, insomnia.
>
> From April 2, 2005, ... I grew worse day by day, I was unable to write, ... and my rigidity would have impeded my driving. To do my work in a hospital, it took more time than usual. I was exhausted.
>
> After learning my diagnosis, it was difficult for me to watch John Paul II on television. However, I felt very close to him in prayer and I knew he could understand what I was going through. I also admired his strength and courage, which motivated me not to give in and to love this suffering, because without love none of this made sense. I can say that it was a daily struggle, but my only

---

[66] Anita S. Bourdin and Sergio Mora, "Up Close With Postulator of John Paul II's Sainthood Cause," an interview with Msgr. Slawamir Oder, Zenit, April 7, 2011, accessed June 13, 2015, https://www.ewtn.com/library/MARY/zpostltrjp2.htm.

wish was to live it with faith and in loving adherence to the will of the Father....

On the afternoon of April 2, the whole community gathered to take part of the Vigil of Prayer in St. Peter's Square, broadcasted live by the French television of the Diocese of Paris.... All of us together heard the announcement of John Paul II's death. At that moment, the world caved in on me. I had lost the friend who understood me and who gave me the strength to keep going. In the following days, I had the sensation of an enormous void, but the certainty of his living presence.

On May 13, the feast of Our Lady of Fatima, Benedict XVI announced the special dispensation to initiate the cause of beatification of John Paul II.[67] Beginning the following day, the sisters of all the French and African communities began to pray for my cure through the intercession of John Paul II. They prayed incessantly until the news arrived of my cure....

On June 1, I was finished; I struggled to stand and to walk. On June 2 in the afternoon, I went to find my superior to ask her if I could leave my work. She asked me to endure a bit longer until my return from Lourdes in August.... Then [she] gave me a pen and told me to write: "John Paul II." It was 5 o'clock in the afternoon. With effort I wrote "John Paul II." ...

---

[67] The minimum waiting period before a petition to open a cause of canonization may be presented to a competent authority is five years after the death of the Servant of God. Congregation for the Causes of Saints, *Norms to Be Observed in Inquiries Made by Bishops in the Causes of Saints*, February 7, 1983, no. 9a.

At 9 o'clock at night, I went to my office before going to my room. I felt ... just as if someone was saying: "Pick up the pen and write." ... To my great surprise I saw that the writing was clearly legible. Not understanding anything, I went to bed.... I woke up at 4:30 a.m., surprised that I was able to sleep, and I leapt out of bed: my body was no longer insensitive, rigid, and interiorly I was not the same.

Then, I felt an interior call and the strong impulse to go to pray before the Most Blessed Sacrament.... I felt a profound peace and a sensation of well being; too great an experience, a mystery difficult to explain in words....

On June 7, as planned, I went to my neurologist, my doctor for the past four years. He was also surprised to see the disappearance of all the symptoms of the disease.[68]

The Healing Power of the Spiritual Works of Mercy

The Spiritual Works of Mercy are as follows:

1. Admonish the sinner.

2. Instruct the ignorant.

3. Counsel the doubtful.

4. Comfort the sorrowful.

---

[68] "Sister Marie Simon-Pierre on Her Cure from Parkinson's," Zenit, April 30, 2011, accessed June 13, 2015, http://www.zenit.org/en/articles/sister-marie-simon-pierre-on-her-cure-from-parkinson.

5. Bear wrongs patiently.

6. Forgive all injuries.

7. Pray for the living and the dead.

We become vessels of healing whenever we engage in the spiritual or Corporal Works of Mercy for the salvation of souls. The spiritual works address a profound need in the soul of humanity to know God in truth. To cease engaging in the works of mercy is to further the work of darkness since such works are a bulwark against the evil one.

Perhaps one of the most challenging works of mercy is the first one: to admonish the sinner. This is increasingly difficult in the broader context of the public square for reasons that Pope Benedict XVI articulated in the book *Light of the World*:

> A new intolerance is spreading, that is quite obvious. There are well-established standards of thinking that are supposed to be imposed on everyone. These are then announced in terms of so-called "negative tolerance." For instance, when people say that for the sake of negative tolerance [i.e., "not offending anyone"] there must be no crucifix in public buildings. With that we are basically experiencing the abolition of tolerance, for it means, after all, that religion, that the Christian faith is no longer allowed to express itself visibly.[69]

As I'm writing this chapter today, June 26, 2015, the United States Supreme Court decided that individual states cannot

---

[69] Pope Benedict XVI, *Light of the World: The Pope, the Church, and the Signs of the Times: A Conversation with Peter Seewald* (San Francisco: Ignatius Press, 2010), 52–53.

prohibit two members of the same sex from contracting civil marriage. Christians have a different understanding of the institution of marriage. The decision of the Supreme Court presents a new challenge to living the gospel. We trust that God will equip the Church with the needed grace to stand firm in truth, but it will become increasingly costly to do so.

"Negative tolerance" also impacts important conversations within our circle of family and friends because everyone can have his own *personal* set of values with freedom to practice whatever he desires as long as no grievous physical harm to others is done, not including the elderly and the unborn. We pray for the courage and wisdom to continue to bear witness to Christ as the Holy Spirit leads. Whether we are peacefully praying in front of an abortion clinic, requiring Catholic schoolteachers to teach authentic Catholicism to our children, or saying Grace at meals in the presence of family members who have left the Church, we risk being ridiculed, criticized, rejected, or called a simpleminded bigot for standing for Christ. Better to risk than to cease living our Catholic identity. And more importantly, there are souls at stake. If we can help save one soul, a great good occurs. Christ calls us to "speak the truth in love," as St. Paul put it (cf. Eph. 4:15).

The lives of the saints exemplify courageous witness, standing for Christ, and never neglecting the Spiritual Works of Mercy. Saints were not necessarily the most popular persons, but the most valiant. As St. Peter taught, "Always be prepared to make a defense to any one who calls you to account for the hope that is in you, yet do it with gentleness and reverence" (1 Pet. 3:15). God is always the initiator of the works of mercy. Healing occurs through the infusion of mercy into the culture. By virtue of our Baptism we are Christ's ambassadors in an anti-Christian world now. Our uniform is a humble garment woven of merciful love and steadfast truth.

Works of Mercy: Healing and Protecting the Culture

In his general audience of November 15, 1972, Pope Paul VI said, "Everything that defends us from sin, protects us from the invisible enemy. Grace is the definitive defense, innocence assumes the aspect of a fortress." As Jesus defended the woman caught in adultery (see John 8:1–11), He defends us. Innocence or purity of heart becomes a fortress of protection against sin and evil. Vessels of divine mercy are soldiers for Christ.

Our strategy against the world, the flesh, and the devil includes defense and offense. The defensive strategy is to live in the state of grace. When we live in obedience to God's law of love and are nurtured by the Word of God, restored by the sacrament of Reconciliation and fed by the Eucharist and personal prayer, our communion with God becomes our defensive shield.

The strategy of offense means we *first* struggle to eliminate the work of the devil and sin *in ourselves*. Then we advance God's kingdom and thwart evil when we help others to break from sin and live in friendship with the Father. Our offense is to proclaim God's extravagant mercy, for we are chosen to lead many to the Father's embrace. We begin at home and then go forth as did the saints.

The power of God's mercy is manifested in foundations such as promoting family, helping Catholics to commit to working in the public square, bringing light into the shady secular work environment, engaging in apostolic work with purity of intention, standing for Christ by an authentic, balanced life that is not duplicitous. We are called to be apostles of mercy who heal the culture by being thoroughly engaged in the Corporal and Spiritual Works of Mercy. We cannot be only consumers of divine mercy. We are sent to heal the secular culture of relativism by the joyful proclamation of God's mercy. These times call for a little army of saints. The Father of Mercy has prepared a people of faith for a time such as this.

Profile in Mercy: St. John Paul II

In January 1945, Edith Zierer, at the age of thirteen, escaped from a Nazi labor camp in Czestochowa, Poland, emaciated and on the verge of death. She was separated from her entire family and was not aware what had happened to them.

Although she could barely walk, she managed to make it to a train station, where she climbed onto a coal wagon. The train moved slowly, but the wind cut through her and the cold became unbearable. She got off the train in a village called Jedrejow, where she sat down in the corner of the station. Edith waited, unable to move, a girl in the striped and numbered uniform of a prisoner, late in an unbearable war. Nobody looked at her.

Death was approaching, but a young man approached first, "very good looking," as she recalled, and vigorous. He wore a long robe and appeared to be a priest. "Why are you here?" he asked. "What are you doing?" Edith said she was trying to get to Kraków to find her parents.

The man disappeared. He came back with a cup of tea. Edith drank. He said he could help her get to Kraków. Again the mysterious benefactor went away, returning with bread and cheese. They talked about the advancing Soviet army. Edith said she believed that her parents and younger sister, Judith, were alive.

"Try to stand," the man said. Edith tried and failed. He carried her to another village, where he put her in the cattle car of a train bound for Kraków. Another family was there. The man got in beside Edith, covered her with his cloak, and made a small fire.

His name, he told Edith, was Karol Wojtyla. Although she took him for a priest, he was still a seminarian who would not be ordained until the next year. Thirty-three more years would pass before he became Pope John Paul II and embarked on a papacy that would help break the Communist hold on Central Europe and so transform the world.

What moved this young seminarian to save the life of a lost Jewish girl cannot be known. But it is clear that his was an act of humanity made as the two great mass movements of the twentieth century, the twin totalitarianisms of fascism and communism, bore down on his nation, Poland.[1]

A twenty-four-year-old Catholic seminarian and a thirteen-year-old Jewish girl were in a ravaged land. Karol

---

[1] See Roger Cohen, "The Polish Seminary Student and the Jewish Girl He Saved," *International Herald Tribune*, April 6, 2005; posted on Dialog, accessed June 27, 2015, http://www.dialog.org/ hist/JohnPaulII-EdithZierer.htm.

Wojtyla had already lost his mother, father, and brother. Unknown yet to Edith, she had already lost her mother at Belzec, her father at Maidanek, and her younger sister at Auschwitz. These two young people, Karol and Edith, could not have been more alone.

The future Polish pope was shaped by such events of his youth and countrymen. The faith of this man of unshakeable conviction moved him to lead the Church with the same heart as he showed to Edith, an abandoned Jewish girl whose life he saved by offering her tea, bread, and shelter when nobody was watching.

Personal or Group Spiritual Exercise

The Teaching of the Word of God
Read the Seven Spiritual Works of Mercy.

1. Admonish the sinner: "[T]here will be more joy in heaven over one sinner who repents than over ninety-nine righteous persons who need no repentance" (Luke 15:7).

2. Instruct the ignorant: "Go into all the world and preach the gospel to the whole creation" (Mark 16:15).

3. To counsel the doubtful: "Peace I leave with you; my peace I give to you. . . . Let not your hearts be troubled" (John 14:27).

4. Comfort the sorrowful: "Come to me, all who labor and are heavy laden, and I will give you rest" (Matt. 11:28).

5. Bear wrongs patiently: "Love your enemies, do good to those who hate you, bless those who curse you" (Luke 6:27–28).

6. Forgive all injuries: "And forgive us our trespasses, as we forgive those who trespass against us" (Matt. 6:12).

7. Pray for the living and the dead: "Father, I desire that they also, whom you have given me, may be with me where I am" (John 17:24).

QUESTIONS FOR GROUP OR PERSONAL REFLECTION

1. Reflect on how you and others have been blessed by engaging in works of mercy. What fruit do you see?

2. Prayerfully consider whether the Lord is asking you to exercise more Spiritual Works of Mercy. How will you respond?

3. Consider the stories of healing in this chapter. How do they speak to your heart?

4. Have you ever been ridiculed, rejected, or persecuted for your Catholic Faith within your circle of friends, family, or coworkers? How did you respond?

5. Do you experience discouragement at the world situation and the persecution of Christians? Ask the Holy Spirit to fill you now with love and courage to strengthen you.

Applying God's Mercy

God's Letter to You

My daughter, know that My Heart is mercy itself. From this sea of mercy, graces flow out upon the whole world. No soul that has approached Me has ever gone away unconsoled. All misery gets buried in the depths of My mercy, and every saving and sanctifying grace flows from this fountain. My daughter, I desire that your heart be an abiding place of My mercy. I desire that this mercy flow out upon the whole world through your heart. Let no one who approaches you go away without that trust in My mercy which I so ardently desire for souls. Pray as much as you can for the dying. By your entreaties, obtain for them trust in My mercy, because they have most need of trust, and have it the least. Be assured that the grace of eternal salvation for certain souls in their final moment depends on your prayer. You know the whole abyss of My mercy, so draw upon it for yourself and especially for poor sinners. Sooner would heaven and earth turn into nothingness than would My mercy not embrace a trusting soul.[70]

---

[70] St. Faustina, *Diary*, no. 1777.

Your Letter to God

Closing Prayers

✝

Anima Christi

Soul of Christ, sanctify me.
Body of Christ, save me.
Blood of Christ, inebriate me.
Water from Christ's side, wash me.
Passion of Christ, strengthen me.
O good Jesus, hear me.
Within Your wounds hide me.
Suffer me not to be separated from You.
From the malicious enemy, defend me.
In the hour of my death, call me
and bid me to come to You
that I may praise You with Your saints
and with Your angels forever and ever. Amen.

Pope Francis Prayer for the Jubilee Year of Mercy

Lord Jesus Christ, you have taught us to be merciful like the
heavenly Father, and have told us that whoever sees you sees

Him. Show us your face, and we will be saved. Your loving gaze freed Zacchaeus and Matthew from being enslaved by money; [freed] the adulteress and Magdalene from seeking happiness only in created things; made Peter weep after his betrayal, and assured Paradise to the repentant thief. Let us hear, as if addressed to each one of us, the words that you spoke to the Samaritan woman: "If you knew the gift of God!" You are the visible face of the invisible Father, of the God who manifests his power above all by forgiveness and mercy: let the Church be your visible face in the world, its Lord risen and glorified. You willed that your ministers would also be clothed in weakness in order that they may feel compassion for those in ignorance and error: let everyone who approaches them feel sought after, loved, and forgiven by God. Send your Spirit and consecrate every one of us with its anointing, so that the Jubilee of Mercy may be a year of grace from the Lord, and your Church, with renewed enthusiasm, may bring good news to the poor, proclaim liberty to captives and the oppressed, and restore sight to the blind. We ask this through the intercession of Mary, Mother of Mercy, you who live and reign with the Father and the Holy Spirit forever and ever. Amen.

Kathleen Beckman, L.H.S.

✠

Kathleen Beckman, L.H.S., is the cofounder and president of the Foundation of Prayer for Priests, an international apostolate for the *spiritual support* of clergy. In conjunction with this apostolate, in 2014, Sophia Institute Press published her book *Praying for Priests: A Mission for the New Evangelization*. An international retreat director and Ignatian-trained spiritual director, Kathleen is the author of several books on the spiritual life emphasizing the healing power of the sacraments and Scripture.

Kathleen hosts the weekly program *Living Eucharist*, which airs internationally on Radio Maria, and has been a frequent guest on EWTN's TV and radio programs.

Since 1991, Kathleen has served in leadership for Magnificat, A Ministry to Catholic Women. Since 2000, she has worked with priests in the ministry of healing and deliverance, and in 2013, she became a spiritual director for the Pope Leo XIII Institute for priests.

In 2001 she was invested into the Equestrian Order of the Holy Sepulchre of Jerusalem. She and her husband are business owners, have two adult sons, and live in Orange, California. Learn more at www.kathleenbeckman.com and www.foundationforpriests.org.

Sophia Institute

Sophia Institute is a nonprofit institution that seeks to nurture the spiritual, moral, and cultural life of souls and to spread the Gospel of Christ in conformity with the authentic teachings of the Roman Catholic Church.

Sophia Institute Press fulfills this mission by offering translations, reprints, and new publications that afford readers a rich source of the enduring wisdom of mankind.

Sophia Institute also operates two popular online Catholic resources: CrisisMagazine.com and CatholicExchange.com.

Crisis Magazine provides insightful cultural analysis that arms readers with the arguments necessary for navigating the ideological and theological minefields of the day. *Catholic Exchange* provides world news from a Catholic perspective as well as daily devotionals and articles that will help you to grow in holiness and live a life consistent with the teachings of the Church.

In 2013, Sophia Institute launched Sophia Institute for Teachers to renew and rebuild Catholic culture through service to Catholic education. With the goal of nurturing the spiritual, moral, and cultural life of souls, and an abiding respect for the role and work of teachers, we strive to provide materials and programs that are at once enlightening to the mind and ennobling to the heart; faithful and complete, as well as useful and practical.

Sophia Institute gratefully recognizes the Solidarity Association for preserving and encouraging the growth of our apostolate over the course of many years. Without their generous and timely support, this book would not be in your hands.

www.SophiaInstitute.com
www.CatholicExchange.com
www.CrisisMagazine.com
www.SophiaInstituteforTeachers.org

Sophia Institute Press® is a registered trademark of Sophia Institute.
Sophia Institute is a tax-exempt institution as defined by the
Internal Revenue Code, Section 501(c)(3). Tax I.D. 22-2548708.